1441

This book is to be returned on or before
the last date stamped below.

WITHDRAWN

Heinemann
ASSEMBLY
Resources

50
Stories
for
ASSEMBLY

David Self

Heinemann

Heinemann Educational Publishers
Halley Court, Jordan Hill, Oxford OX2 8EJ
a division of Reed Educational & Professional Publishing Ltd

OXFORD FLORENCE PRAGUE MADRID ATHENS
MELBOURNE AUCKLAND KUALA LUMPUR SINGAPORE
TOKYO IBADAN NAIROBI KAMPALA JOHANNESBURG
GABORONE PORTSMOUTH NH (USA) CHICAGO
MEXICO CITY SAO PAULO

Text © David Self, 1997

First published 1997

97 98 99 00 01 10 9 8 7 6 5 4 3 2 1

British Library Cataloguing in Publication Data

A catalogue record for this book is available from the British Library

ISBN 0 435 30249 3

Designed by Mike Brain, Oxford
Cover illustration by Balvir Koura
Typeset by Books Unlimited (Nottm) NG19 7QZ
Printed and bound in Great Britain by Biddles Ltd, Guildford

The publishers would like to thank E. Huda Bladon for reading and
commenting on the Muslim stories in this book.

FOR CELIA, FIONA AND GEOFF

Contents

Introduction

THE PRIMARY SCHOOL headteacher stood up and beamed at her assembled pupils. 'Now, it's the beginning of a new term. I want you to have a happy term and Jesus wants you to have a happy term. But I won't have a happy term and you won't have a happy term and Jesus won't have a happy term if you climb on the toilet roof.'

Ever since I first heard that story some fifteen years ago, I've enjoyed it for a variety of reasons. It reminds me of a particular headteacher I once knew. It illustrates the agonizing balancing act that must be achieved by teachers forced to use 'school assembly' for the conduct of school business while observing the legal requirement to hold an 'act of worship'; and it's a reminder of many well-intentioned assemblies that almost came right.

Interestingly, since I first quoted the story in a book published in 1982, it has been retold to me on several occasions as having happened in recent assemblies in specific schools. It has become the educational equivalent of a modern, urban myth. So is it true?

That is the wrong question.

The proper question to ask about any story is, 'What truth does it contain?' (The answer, in this case, is that it's horribly easy to get 'assembly' wrong.)

Some of the stories in this book are true: they record comparatively recent history. Provided I have not made any ghastly errors of fact, these are 'literally' true, although different readers and listeners may dispute the 'angle' from which I may have described a given incident. Other stories are 'true' for the members of the tradition from which those particular stories come. Some may be no more than legends or myths for most readers and listeners. And there will be some stories which are 'gospel' or 'revealed truth' to some hearers but which will be fantasy to others in the same audience.

As Jack Priestley wrote, though, in *The Junior RE Handbook* (Stanley Thornes, 1990): 'Religious stories are not scientific accounts. They are part of the biographies of those who try to live them out.' So it is hoped that *all* these stories will 'contain a truth' for all those who hear them.

For the purpose of this collection is to help children both to learn about and to learn from religion (two Religious Education Attainment Targets as outlined by the School Curriculum and Assessment Authority). The stories therefore, first describe key places and 'key points in the life stories of important religious figures' that will be encountered in many Key Stage 2 programmes of study. It is hoped too that they 'show that religion is important to some people and affects their daily lives' (that is, the stories provide examples of religious commitment). Secondly, these stories are intended to help listeners to develop an appreciation of moral values, and to make comparisons between significant experiences of others and their own emotions and experiences. Put more simply, the stories celebrate religious idealism and commitment, and will help to nurture a sense of idealism and an awareness of the individuality of others.

In practical terms, it is hoped that the stories will also answer the requirement of the 1988 Education Reform Act for schools to hold daily 'acts of collective worship' which are 'wholly or mainly of a broadly Christian character' – even though that Act begs such questions as 'What is meant by "mainly"?' 'How "broad" is "broad"?' And, indeed, the question whether you can make a child 'worship'. For if we are realistic, we must agree that a school act of worship (at its best) can do no more than provide an *opportunity* for worship. Whatever some politicians might like to believe, worship (which is a state of mind, not simply a posture) cannot be enforced.

Many teachers have taken heart from one reading of the Act which suggests that so long as a *majority* of assemblies are 'Christian', then the Act is being observed. Increasingly (and with the support of some senior church people) it is being argued that the law contains within itself considerable flexibility: schools can use it to develop collective 'spiritual' acts which, in their broadness, leave space for all pupils to 'explore their own beliefs'. So, while the majority of the stories here come from the Christian tradition, the book also includes narratives from the other world faith communities.

The stories can be used in a variety of ways. Most obviously, they may simply be read (or, better, 'told' – see below) as 'stories for assembly'; they provide the opportunity for a group or year or whole school to come together to share and enjoy the same experience. To this end, two introductions have been provided for each story. The first is a background note for the assembly leader's information. The second may serve as a ready-made introduction which can simply be read aloud to introduce the story to its audience when time does not permit the devising of a more locally relevant introduction. Some of the longer stories may be used in two parts.

Alternatively, the stories can be used as part of the Religious Education curriculum, especially at Key Stage 2. Here they might provide a springboard for discussion, for work in art and drama and as a stimulus to the writing of further (more personal) stories. Some of the stories in this book might also provide an RE element in project work. For example, stories 28, 43 and 47 could have a place in a project or topic on food; numbers 9, 10, and 11 in one on the Romans; numbers 11, 17, 32 and 34 in one on poverty or 'sharing'; and numbers 1, 2 and 50 in one on leadership.

Classroom work may be fed back into 'whole school' assemblies which are presented by one class – and many of the stories will lend themselves to dramatised readings by several voices.

This collection is offered only as a resource, not as a course of ready-made assemblies. The appropriate atmosphere (in which, for example, stillness and quietness have their place) cannot be created by a mere book. Nor is it suggested that any assembly leader work steadily through this anthology, day by day or week by week. Nor will every story be suitable in every context. As the 1988 Act reminds us, any materials must be 'appropriate having regard to the family background, ages and aptitudes of the pupils involved'. I do not therefore imagine that every user of the book will wish to endorse (and consequently read) every story it contains. I hope, however, that whoever uses this anthology will find plenty of stories which will engage those who hear them.

There are fewer 'Bible' stories than might be expected since there is no shortage of 'children's Bibles' and similar story books on the market. Those I have included are, I hope, both relevant and fresh. I have also made a deliberate attempt to introduce stories about women in what is frequently an all-male world or subject.

Stories from the Judaeo-Christian tradition come first in the book, arranged chronologically. These are followed by stories from the other world faiths. Throughout the book, the terms BCE (Before the Common Era) and CE have been preferred to BC and AD. Some of the Islamic stories mention the name of the Prophet, Muhammad. Muslims are enjoined (when speaking his name) to follow it with a blessing: 'Peace and blessings be upon him.' Those retelling these stories should decide whether it is appropriate in their circumstances to follow this custom.

Many of the stories were originally written for either the BBC School Radio assembly series, *Together*, or for the RE series, *Contact* and *Quest*. Others were written for the BBC Television programmes, *Knock, Knock* and *Umbrella*. Consequently, their style is deliberately conversational rather than literary – as is the style of those stories written especially for this collection. This 'spoken voice' should help those who read them aloud to 'share' them with their listeners rather than merely vocalising the words.

Where relevant, some thought might be given as to who would be the best available reader (or readers) for any particular story. In any case, some rehearsal is advisable before any reading. No matter how much at home you feel reading to an assembly, remember that even a professional actor or reader prefers to have time to rehearse; that is, to check that he or she understands the meaning of what is to be read, to absorb its mood and tone, to appreciate the viewpoint of the narrative; and to note where pauses and changes of pace are necessary. Some phonetic pronunciations have been provided for unusual names. Square brackets surround references to other stories: such allusions may be omitted if those listening have not yet heard the story being cross-referenced.

The gathering together of a number of people for assembly places a heavy responsibility on those who lead that assembly.

I hope this collection will lighten the load a little and help the arrangement of assemblies (or even acts of worship) which nurture an awareness of the transcendent and the needs of others; which develop a sense of community and of what it means to be religious; and which create a feeling of wonder, mystery, joy and (especially) idealism.

DAVID SELF

1

The reluctant leader

While Jews consider Abraham to be the father or patriarch of their race, it was Moses who led them out of Egypt, who received the law on Mount Sinai and who shaped their nation. Yet he, the greatest of Jewish leaders, was reluctant to take up the role, as is recorded in chapter 3 of the biblical book of Exodus.

Besides teaching something of the life of Moses, this story is about leadership – its responsibilities and requirements. What makes a good leader, be it a classroom monitor or the ruler of a country?

Some people want to boss everything. Whether it's a soccer team or just a group of their friends forming a new club or gang. Up goes their hand. 'Me! Me, I'll do it. I'll be captain. I'll be the leader. Go on, let me…'

That doesn't mean he or she will turn out to be a good leader. The person who would make the best leader may be keeping quiet. And other people may not think of him or her as a possible leader. Indeed, he or she may not want to be leader. Some people really dread the idea; hate the thought of having to be 'in charge'. 'Oh no,' they say. 'Not me. Someone else. So-and-so's good at organising people. Let them do it.'

So what's it like if you don't want to be a leader – but you're forced into it? Like when a teacher's going to be out of the classroom for a while. 'Right, now while I'm out, I'm leaving Verity in charge. She's sensible – so you must all do what she says.' And that's the last thing Verity wants. She hates speaking up, hates having to be the boss.

◆

YEARS AND YEARS ago – well, centuries and centuries ago to be more accurate, it was just the same for Moses. Except in his case, it was God who insisted he be a leader. Leader of all the Jewish people. And what's more, God told Moses he'd got to arrange for all the Jews to escape from Egypt. Not an easy job!

The reason they were all in Egypt was because, a long time before this, there had been a famine in their own land. None of the crops had grown and, as a result, they had nothing to eat. The Jews had to travel in search of food. Eventually they arrived in this country called Egypt where there was plenty to eat. But there was a price to pay!

The Egyptians made the Jews work as their slaves, doing all sorts of tiring tasks. What's more, they treated them very harshly and cruelly.

Now Moses (who was, of course, a Jew) had an easier job than some. He worked as a shepherd, looking after some sheep that belonged to his father-in-law. One day, when he was out on a hillside with the sheep, he suddenly noticed an amazing sight. A bush. On fire. Now, there's nothing especially amazing about that – except that the flames weren't destroying the bush. It was burning without being eaten up by the fire. Moses went closer to see what it was. And as he did, he heard a voice coming from the burning bush. And Moses knew at once that it was God speaking to him.

God told Moses how he wanted him to be the leader of the Jewish people. He was to speak to the ruler of Egypt (who was called the Pharaoh) and to say that he, the Pharaoh, was to let the Jews leave Egypt. The thought of doing this terrified Moses.

'Why me?' he said. 'I'd be a useless leader.'

'Don't worry,' said the voice of God. 'I'll be with you. I'll give you strength.'

'But the Jewish people won't believe I'm to be their leader. They won't accept me as their leader.'

'You must tell them that I, the Lord God, have given you authority to be their leader.'

'But,' said Moses, still worked up at the thought of having to do all this, 'even if the Jewish people accept me, the Egyptians won't do what I say.'

'I shall give you power,' said the Lord God, 'power to perform signs which will convince the Pharaoh and all the Egyptians.'

'What do you mean? "Signs"?'

'What's that in your hand?' asked God.

'My stick. I use it to chase away any dog that comes after the sheep.'

'Throw it on the ground,' said God.

So Moses did what he was told – and, immediately, the stick turned into a wriggling snake. Moses started to run away.

'Don't do that,' said God. 'Pick it up by the tail.'

Moses wasn't too keen on doing that but he knew that he must trust God. So, very nervously, he went back to where the snake was still wriggling and stretched out his hand. And as soon as he plucked up courage to seize its tail, it turned back into a stick.

'That's what I mean by a sign,' said God. 'I shall give you powers that will persuade the people.'

'But I'll still be useless as a leader,' replied Moses. 'I'm no good ☛

at persuading people, getting them to do what I say. I'm hopeless at speaking in public — '

'Don't worry. I'll be with you. And your brother, Aaron, will help. He's a good talker. You'll tell him what to say and he'll speak out all right...'

And that's what happened. Moses, who felt he was the last person on this earth to be a leader, became one of the most famous leaders in all history.

The Jewish people did what he said; he persuaded the Pharaoh (in the end) to let them all leave Egypt – and Moses was able to lead them to freedom in their own country. God had not, after all, asked him to do something impossible. But how Moses did it, well, that's another story. ◆

2

Let us go

This reading continues the story of Moses. Rather than concentrating on the well-known story of the Passover when, as the Book of Exodus tells us, the Angel of Death killed the Egyptian first-born but 'passed over' the children of the Israelites (an event commemorated each year by Jewish people at Passover), the story features the 'bargaining' between Moses and the Egyptian Pharaoh that led up to this, and emphasises Moses' commitment to the purpose God gave him. (Links may also be made with the Ten Commandments: see Exodus chapters 19 and 20.)

You remember the story of Moses? How God chose him to be the leader of the Jewish people and to help them escape from Egypt? Even though he thought he would be useless as a leader? Well, this is the story of how God helped Moses to persuade the Egyptians to let the Jews (or Israelites as they were sometimes called) leave that country.

And despite all the setbacks, Moses never gave up. He knew now what he was supposed to do – and he stuck at it!

Remember: on one side in this struggle are the Israelites, eager to escape from slavery in Egypt; on the other, are the Egyptians, keen to keep hold of these useful, low-paid workers.

◆

MOSES, THE NEW leader of the Israelites, was standing in front of the Egyptian ruler, the Pharaoh, in his palace. But Moses wasn't alone. Beside him stood his brother, Aaron. There was a long, long silence.

'So what is it you want?' boomed the Pharaoh at last.

Moses was so nervous he could do little more than mumble. ☛

'Speak up, speak up,' ordered the Pharaoh. 'I haven't got all day. Well, I *have* got all day. To do just what I like – and I don't want to spend it listening to two immigrant slaves.'

Moses turned and whispered to Aaron. 'You tell him. You said you would.'

Aaron whispered back. 'What do you want me to say?'

'He's to let us go.'

'I'm to what?' said the Pharaoh, overhearing what they were saying.

Aaron plucked up his courage. 'Lord Pharaoh, we speak – that is, I'm speaking on behalf of my brother here —'

'On behalf of our people,' whispered Moses.

'Yes, on behalf of our people. Our Lord God of Israel says that the Pharaoh must let our people go —'

'Why should I?'

Aaron turned to Moses. 'Why?' he asked in another whisper.

'To worship Him.'

'Lord Pharaoh, to worship God. To hold a feast in his honour. In the desert. God'll be angry with us if we don't obey his command.'

'And I'll be angry with you, Moses, if I hear any more of this,' said the Pharaoh to Aaron.

At this, Moses at last spoke up. '*I'm* Moses. He's my brother Aaron.'

'Oh!' said the Pharaoh. 'So *you're* Moses. A silent leader. Well, it makes no difference.'

And he signalled to the guards to remove the two of them

from the palace. But that wasn't the end of it because the Pharaoh (who was called Ramases II) issued a new instruction. From that day, the Israelite slaves (whose job it was to work as builders for the Egyptians) were no longer to be supplied with materials with which to make bricks. From then on, they had to find their own materials – and still make the same number of bricks each day.

That meant a much harder life for the Israelite people, but it was also the start of a whole series of troubles for the Egyptians.

Because it was then that the signs began. Signs a bit like the time that Moses' stick had turned into a snake.

First the River Nile became polluted and its waters became the colour of blood. And of course the whole country depended on the river. For travelling. To water the crops. For drinking-water. So the Egyptians were in trouble. Then, because of the pollution, there came a plague of frogs. They were everywhere. Escaping from the river. And then the other plagues started. Plagues of gnats, plagues of flies – all feeding on the fish killed by the pollution.

The next disaster happened when disease struck the cattle which used to drink from the river. And then people began to get ill. Skin troubles. All sorts of things.

After each disaster, Moses and Aaron visited the Pharaoh's palace to beg that the Israelite people may go into the desert to worship their God. On each occasion, he listened to them and, in return, asked for Egypt to be set free from each disaster. 'Take this plague away from us and I, Pharaoh of Egypt, agree to let you and your people go into the desert to worship your god.'

But, as soon as each plague had ended, the Pharaoh changed his ☛

mind. Even so, Moses didn't give up. Back he went, after each of the plagues, to try to get the Pharaoh to change his mind.

Then, finally, came three days' darkness in what was usually the hot and sunny land of Egypt. Yet again, Moses went back to the Pharaoh.

'For three days, the light of the sun has been blotted out. Yes?'

'I know!' said the Pharaoh, grumpily.

'Clouds so dark it's been impossible to see a man standing next to you?' Moses stopped for a moment, then tried again. 'It's a sign. A sign, from God. He wants —'

'All right, all right, you've made your point,' interrupted the Pharaoh. 'You can leave the city. Go into the desert to worship ... to worship your "god". You, your children, all of the Israelites, yes.'

'And our animals,' added Moses.

'Ah! No. No, they stay here.'

'But our cattle must go with us. We need them.'

'I know exactly why you need them. Because you're not planning to return. After worshipping your "god" you'll be off, out into the desert and we'll be without any slaves. Now, get out of here. You'll never be allowed to see me again.'

And Moses and the Pharaoh never did meet again. But the Israelites *were* to be allowed out of Egypt. That happened when many Egyptian children died, all in the same night; a night when no Israelite children died. Only then did the Pharaoh let the Israelites (that is, the Jewish people) go. And so they left Egypt, led by Moses – a man who, despite his worries, always trusted in God. And it was Moses who was later to give God's commandments to the people: the ten commandments which still teach us today what is right and what is wrong. ◆

3

A *stranger in a strange land*

This is a retelling of the story of Ruth, who is the subject of the eighth book of the Old Testament (and great-grandmother of King David). A short romantic tale, it tells how Ruth leaves her own land to care for her widowed mother-in-law, Naomi, in Bethlehem. The moral of the story as told in the Bible is one of religious tolerance: Ruth may be a foreigner but she fulfils the Jewish law. As the story is retold here, it emphasises the quality of being prepared to put the needs of others before one's immediate desires.

I'll tell you straight away: this is a story which ends happily ever after. But it's a story about bad news as well as good news. It's about a young woman called Ruth who has to face all sorts of dangers and problems – but it's not just a story about Ruth.

It's a reminder that one day, when you're all grown up, there'll come a time when it's your responsibility to care for your parents – just as they care for you now.

◆

WELL, FIRST CAME the bad news; then the good news. Then more bad news, followed by more ... bad news. One thing after another, that's what it seemed like to Naomi.

It all began with the famine. A really serious lack of food in the land then called Palestine. [Just like the time, many hundreds of years before, when another famine had sent the people who lived there in those days in search of food in Egypt.]

And this [new] famine was especially bad around a little town called Bethlehem. And that's where Naomi lived with her husband Elimelech [*say:* ee-lim-e-leck] and their two growing ☛

sons. Eventually, they decided there was nothing for it. They would have to leave their home and go in search of food. So off they set, travelling eastwards, across the River Jordan to a foreign country, known as the Land of Moab [*say:* mo-ab].

They may have been strangers and foreigners in that land but they still found food and somewhere to live – so that was the good news. And the two boys grew up and married local Moabite girls called Orpah and Ruth. And that was more good news. But it was then that things went wrong again.

First, Elimelech died. And (to make it much worse) so, too, did his two sons. That left Naomi, Orpah and Ruth – all three – without husbands. In those days it was almost impossible for a family to survive without a husband or father. If you'd no family to look after you, well, that was just bad luck.

So Naomi, who was now getting quite old, decided she would rather go back to her own country where she had friends, especially as she had heard there was no longer a famine in the countryside around Bethlehem.

So the three of them started out together. They hadn't gone far when Naomi stopped. 'Listen,' she said to Orpah and Ruth. 'You must stay in your own country. That's where you belong and you're still young enough to find new husbands.' Neither of them wanted to leave Naomi but, in the end, Orpah decided she'd stay in her own country. Ruth, however, thought otherwise. 'Don't ask me to leave you. Wherever you go, I'll go. Wherever you want to live, I'll live. You looked after me when I was young, now it's my turn to look after you.'

Naomi knew she wasn't going to change Ruth's mind so, after Orpah went back to Moab, the two of them travelled on together. Ruth was determined to help her mother-in-law,

Naomi, but felt unsure what it would be like to be a stranger in a strange land.

———————

They arrived back in Bethlehem in April, at the time of the barley harvest. And even though Naomi was glad to be back and to see her old friends again, she had her worries. She did not know how two widows – a mother and her grown-up daughter-in-law – might earn a living.

But there was a law in those days which allowed poor people to pick up all the waste ears of corn and barley that were dropped on the ground at harvest time.

So Ruth spent her time walking behind the people who were gathering in the harvest, feeling very lonely, very much on her own, but picking up anything they dropped – ready to take it back to Naomi to use to make bread.

One day, the rich man who owned all the fields round there noticed Ruth. Boaz, as he was called, spoke to his foreman. 'Who's that handsome young woman, over there?'

The man answered, 'She's that foreign girl, the one who came back from the Land of Moab to help look after Naomi.' Now Boaz was a distant relative of Naomi, so he went over to Ruth and told her that, when she was hungry or thirsty, she could eat and drink with his workers.

Ruth was surprised. 'Why should you be so kind to a stranger?' Boaz told her how he knew about the death of her husband and her father, and how she had come to what was, to her, a foreign country to look after Naomi. 'For what you've done, you deserve a reward.'

And later that afternoon, he secretly told his workers to drop some barley or corn on purpose – so Ruth would have all the more to take home. ☞

11

That night Ruth told Naomi all that had happened. And that was what gave Naomi an idea – because in those days, there was another law which said that if a woman's husband died, her close relatives should look after her. But was Ruth a really close relative of Boaz? Would the law apply to her? Would Boaz look after Ruth when Naomi died and when Ruth really would be all on her own?

So Naomi decided to send Ruth to Boaz and ask him if he would indeed look after her when the time came, perhaps giving her a job as a servant. When Boaz heard what Ruth was asking, he thought for a moment and then said he would have to make certain arrangements.

And what were those arrangements? Well, they were only for a wedding – a wedding between himself and Ruth! So, after all the bad news, here was more good news. Ruth was happy; Boaz was happy (because he liked Ruth and he knew that she was a loving, caring person); and old Naomi was happy because she now knew that, after all, her daughter-in-law was not going to end up as a stranger in a strange land.

Ruth was not only pleased for herself: she was happy her mother-in-law had no more worries in her old age. She now also understood that, although things seemed to have gone wrong in the past, God had not forgotten her. She'd been lonely, yes, but she'd never been *alone*. But because she *had* known what it was like to be lonely, she now appreciated just how good it was to have kind friends and a kind husband once again. ◆

David and Goliath

David's name appears more than 1000 times in the Bible: he is presented (usually) as the ideal Hebrew king, although there are enough 'human' stories about him for him also to appear a convincing character. That said, it is impossible to say for certain which parts of the Old Testament narrative are fact and which are idealised legend.

We are told he was the son of Jesse of Bethlehem; that he was anointed by the prophet Samuel to be successor to Saul, the first king of Israel; and that he worked as a shepherd for his father. 'He was ruddy, and had beautiful eyes, and was handsome.'

This is a story about a war, and also a story about a hero. It's about a young boy (called David) who trusted in God and who showed great courage when his country was being attacked by a powerful enemy – even when his own side's army was ready to give up. It's also a story about a giant – and a story that proves young people (as well as grown-ups) can be courageous and brave.

◆

IT ALL HAPPENED 3000 years ago, in the land of Israel; the land where the Jewish people had settled after their escape from slavery in Egypt; a land where they had lived and farmed peacefully for many years.

Except that now it was being attacked. The Philistines had invaded from the north and their mighty army had moved south, seizing the land it occupied. And now the two armies were facing each other, in the valley of the river Elah, about fifteen miles west of the little town of Bethlehem.

I say 'armies' but the Israelites weren't proper soldiers: they ☞

were mostly farmers who had just joined together to try to defend their land. They had few horses so they had to fight on foot. Some had swords and shields but most had to rely on wooden clubs. A few had slingshots. These were leather cups with two thongs or straps attached to them. You put a stone in the leather cup, held the two thongs and whirled it round your head. Then you let go of one thong and out flew the stone. They were used by shepherds when wolves attacked their sheep. Some men could hit a wolf at 50 metres.

But the Philistine army had horses, chariots and proper armour. And, what's more, their iron swords were better than those of the Israelites. They were also taller and bigger men. And the plumed helmets that they wore made them look even bigger. So, although the Israelites were keen to defend their land, they weren't too keen on fighting the Philistines. Especially as they'd heard stories about one of the Philistines, a real giant of a man called Goliath – who came from a place called Gath.

One morning, Goliath issued a challenge. 'So what are you doing here, you Israelites? Are you going to fight or not? I'll tell you what: to save you *all* from being killed, choose one of your men – anyone – and we'll fight. Just him and me. And if he wins and kills me, we'll be your slaves. But if I win and kill him, well, you'll become our slaves.'

Even though this would save a lot of bloodshed, the Israelites weren't very keen on the idea. 'I'd rather be a slave than dead,' said one of them.

'What chance have we got?' asked another. 'He's twice the height of an ordinary man.'

So the King of the Israelites, King Saul, made a promise to his men. 'If one of you fights and kills Goliath, I'll give him a reward.'

Still no-one volunteered. So Saul made another offer. 'And he shall have my daughter to marry.'

Again, no volunteers. So Saul made yet another offer. 'And his family need pay no tax for the rest of his life.'

Even then no-one volunteered. And every day Goliath repeated his challenge.

Now, in the Israelite army were several brothers, all sons of a man called Jesse who lived near Bethlehem. And every so often their much younger brother came to where the army was in camp – bringing food for his older brothers. Mainly bread and cheese was what he brought and he was called David. He was still a boy but he was old enough to look after his father's sheep while his elder brothers were away.

Well, one particular day, he arrived just after Goliath had repeated his challenge and all the men were still talking about it. David wanted to know what it was all about and, as soon as he'd heard, he went straight to King Saul – and volunteered. 'But you can't fight him. You're just a boy and he's an experienced soldier.'

'God will protect me,' said David.

'Well, God go with you then,' said Saul. When they tried the king's own armour on David it was far too big. Far too heavy. David could hardly move in it, never mind fight.

'I'll go as I am,' he said. So he took his shepherd's stick and chose five smooth pebbles from a nearby brook. He put them in a purse that he wore round his waist and with his shepherd's sling in his hand, he walked towards Goliath. ☞

When Goliath saw him approaching, he laughed. 'Am I a dog that you come at me with just a stick?'

David carried on walking.

'Come any nearer and you'll be dead,' said Goliath.

David stopped, still some distance away from Goliath. He took a pebble, put it in his sling and took aim. The pebble hit Goliath straight on the forehead with such force it knocked him unconscious and he fell to the ground. David ran towards him, seized the huge man's sword and, with it, killed him.

When they saw what had happened, the Philistine army fled (rather than become the slaves of the Israelites). And when the Israelites saw what had happened, they cheered and cheered. King Saul welcomed David back to the camp and, from then on, David lived with Saul's family. He became a close friend of Saul's son, Jonathan, and was a popular hero in the eyes of all the people of Israel. David, who wasn't afraid and who trusted in God. ◆

5

David the Psalmist

Following the defeat of Goliath, David became Saul's armour-bearer, a captain over Saul's fighting men, the beloved friend of Jonathan – and the husband of Saul's daughter, Michal. But eventually, because of his ever-increasing popularity and Saul's jealousy, he had to flee the court (as this story tells).

The story will also serve as an introduction to one or more of the Psalms which form part of the Hebrew scriptures and the Old Testament. They are often called 'the Psalms of David' because he was a skilled singer and player of the lyre but, while his name does stand at the head of many of them, he was not necessarily the author of even those ones. Many could, however, have been written from his experiences.

This is the story about a brave soldier called David. [You'll remember the story of how he defeated the giant Philistine, Goliath.] He became very popular with the Israelite people and was later to become their king but, at the time of this story, Saul was king and David was just a captain in Saul's army. However, David had also married Saul's daughter, Michal [his reward for defeating Goliath].

There was another thing about David: he was a great musician and singer. He is said to have written many songs, songs that we now call the Psalms – and this is a story about David the Psalmist.

◆

DAVID THE PSALMIST, yes. But our story begins with Saul. King Saul. And he was not only king, he was a powerful and victorious king. He'd defeated his enemies, the Philistines. Everything was going well for him – so he should have been in a good mood. But he wasn't. He was in a foul mood as he stomped around his palace, muttering to himself.

'I feel as if ... as if I'm being attacked. Attacked, yes, as if I was a cornered army. This mood, it's like some cloud of poison that surrounds me.'

It was his son Jonathan who first came up with the idea. 'Father,' he said, 'some people say music is the best thing to cheer you up.'

'Then bring me music,' snapped Saul. And Jonathan knew exactly who the musician was that could cheer up Saul. David, who'd been a shepherd boy. [David, who'd killed the Philistine giant, Goliath.] David, who played an instrument a bit like a small harp, called a lyre.

Jonathan led him in to King Saul. 'Ahh!' said the king. 'So you play the lyre as well as everything else?'

David was modest. 'Your majesty, I have some skill.'

'So what do you play?' asked the king.

'Songs I make up mostly. In praise of God.'

And so David became official musician to Saul and played his lyre whenever Saul wanted. Even so, as time went by, David began to feel that the king did not really like him. Jonathan tried to reassure David. 'You cheer him up. Whenever you play.' David wasn't so sure. Jonathan tried again. 'The people like you. You're popular.' But that was the trouble. The people did like David, so much so that Saul was becoming jealous of David. What's more, he'd started plotting against him.

One day when David was away from the royal court, Saul told Jonathan what he was planning. 'I've decided to kill David.' At first, Jonathan just laughed. It sounded so ... weird. But Jonathan soon realised that Saul wasn't joking.

'But father...,' he pleaded, 'don't harm David. Please! For me.

For *you*. He's not done anything wrong. It's the opposite. He makes music for you. Whenever that mood comes upon you, he cheers you up.'

'He's too popular. He's the people's hero.'

'He's loyal to you. He is! [Think how he risked his life in fighting Goliath.]'

Saul seemed convinced by what Jonathan said so Jonathan began to think that his father wouldn't really harm David. Even so, he warned his friend. Secretly. And David promised to be on his guard. What's more, he was sure he'd be safe.

'I'll be all right. Remember that song I made up? "The Lord is my shepherd, I have everything I need... Even though I walk through the deepest darkness, I will not be afraid because You, God, are with me."'

So David went to play his lyre for Saul – and Saul sat listening. And while he played, David kept an eye on Saul. But suddenly, the evil mood came upon Saul again and, with one quick movement, Saul seized a spear and threw it straight at David.

David saw it in time and dodged it. The spear stuck in the wall, just where David had been. In a second, David was out of the room. At first he hid in his own room but news came that Saul's soldiers were searching for him. His wife, Michal, helped him to escape out of a window and then she put a statue in David's bed to make it look as if he was still asleep.

All this gave David time to get away from Saul's soldiers and to escape into the countryside. It was there that he was able to meet his friend Jonathan again.

Jonathan wanted to go back and plead with Saul but David knew Saul wouldn't have him back. So what was David going ☛

to do now? 'I'll live here, here in the hills. I'll find food. The Lord God will protect me. "He'll prepare a banquet for me."'

Jonathan recognised the words. 'That's from that song of yours. You sing even when you're alone, don't you?'

'Mm,' said David, 'I sing when I feel lonely. To remind me God always helps those who do what He wants. The words came to me when I was young and looking after my father's sheep. Just as I was their shepherd, so the Lord God is my shepherd. Like the sheep, I've everything I need. "He lets me rest in fields of green grass and leads me to quiet pools of fresh water. He gives me new strength, he guides me in the right paths, as he has promised."'

Jonathan never forgot those words which are part of one of the songs we call the Psalms; and they're still sung today by people who feel, as David did, that God cares for those who follow his teaching. ◆

6

Mephibosheth

Mephibosheth must be one of the least known characters in the Old Testament. He was the son of David's friend, Jonathan and the grandson of King Saul. When the throne passed to David, Mephibosheth (along with other members of Saul's family) were 'marginalized'. This story is loosely developed from references to Mephibosheth in 2 Samuel, chapter 4, verse 4 and 2 Samuel, chapter 9, verse 1. Besides picturing an interesting Biblical character, it teaches something about what it is like to cope with disability – and how we might regard those who have a disability.

Have you ever been told to 'go and see' someone, someone important or a bit frightening? Perhaps you've been told 'to go and see the headteacher' – and you didn't know why! Inside, you felt all nervous: were you going to be told off? Had you done something wrong which you didn't know about?

This is a story of a boy in the Bible who was told he must go and report to someone really important. He was told he had to go to the royal palace because the king wanted to see him. As we'll hear, he had good reason to be afraid – and he also had another problem: he was lame.

His name was Mephibosheth [*say:* muh-fib-oh-sheth].

◆

MEPHIBOSHETH WAS SCARED. Not that excited, giggly feeling you get when you're not sure what's going to happen next but you hope it might be something quite nice after all…

No, really scared. All sort of empty in his stomach and numb. And feeling real trouble must be about to happen, trouble he wouldn't be able to cope with. ☛

21

He'd been sent a message that he was to go to see the king. King David himself, in his palace! In Jerusalem! All right, so having to go to see someone important can make you nervous, but what was making him *scared* was that the last time any of his family were sent for like this, they didn't come back...

He was only young when that had happened and he hadn't understood what it was all about. The grown-ups wouldn't explain but it was something to do with things that had happened in the war. Two of his uncles and five cousins had been sent for, they went to the palace ... and were never seen or heard of again. They just 'disappeared'.

Mephibosheth had almost no relatives. His father was killed in that same war when he was five. And the war was why he had two legs that just wouldn't support his weight. A cripple, some thoughtless people called him. During the war, news had come that his father and grandfather had been killed and the fighting was getting closer. Everyone said the family should try to escape. He was only five at the time and, as they were then a rich family, he was being looked after by a nurse. Well, she picked him up and started to run but she managed to drop him. It wasn't funny. Somehow, both his ankles broke and there wasn't time to set the bones properly so they'd healed all wrong and ever since he had had to use crutches. He couldn't join in games with other boys and he became the one who was always left out. 'The boy who was different.'

As he grew up, he was looked after by people who'd known his father. They were sorry for him but they also thought he was a nuisance, something they wished they'd never taken on. He'd never be able to join the army and he wouldn't be able to farm the land, not properly... But then, out of the blue, came this message.

What I haven't told you yet is that he was the grandson of Saul, who was king before King David. And Saul and David had not always been the best of friends! So did King David now think of Saul's grandson as an enemy?

But Mephibosheth's father, whose name had been Jonathan, had been a great friend of David. Then David became king but after the war there was that business about his uncles and cousins – and Saul was dead and Jonathan was dead... So, one way and another, Mephibosheth had grown up having nothing to do with palace life and court officials. He was no longer King Saul's grandson, he was just 'the cripple lad who can't do a proper day's work'. Until he got that message.

So Mephibosheth went to Jerusalem. To see the king. If you say it like that, it sounds easy. What really happened was, he spent three days talking to different people in the village, trying to persuade one of the farmers to lend him a donkey on which to ride there. You couldn't blame them for not wanting to lend him one. I don't think anyone expected ever to see Mephibosheth again. But in the end, yes, one old man did lend him his donkey. Poor creature, it was hardly up to the journey any more than Mephibosheth was, but off they went.

Mephibosheth didn't have *all* that much trouble finding people who'd help him get on and off the donkey, but it's amazing how many people are nervous of touching someone who's disabled. Yet somehow he eventually arrived in Jerusalem and then it all seemed suddenly much more frightening.

Jerusalem was a very busy place and everyone seemed to know where they were going. Except Mephibosheth. He had to ask the way; and it sounded daft saying, 'Excuse me, could you tell me the way to the king's palace?' – when he was heaving him- ☞

self along on crutches, with an ancient donkey limping along behind him.

But, eventually, he found his way there – and the palace guards, huge men in armour, well, they seemed to be expecting him, which made it worse. Someone led the donkey away to give it water and he was left to wait for what seemed like three days. He kept thinking what they could do to him. Beat him? Put him in prison? Something even worse? He tried to practise things to say, like 'Thank you for asking me.' 'Please have mercy on me, I haven't done anything wrong and I was only a young boy when all that other business happened...'

Then he was sent for. That walk! That *hobble*! Along a huge corridor... Then he was in a big room. The king was there. Mephibosheth felt he was swaying. He tried to bow but the shiny, polished floor caused him to drop one of his crutches. It clattered to the ground. He bent down, trying to pick it up ... and then the king came towards him. King David. And *he* bent down and picked it up and gave it to Mephibosheth. And he smiled.

'Mephibosheth,' he said, and Mephibosheth couldn't say anything. But David must have known how his visitor felt because he said, 'Don't be afraid.' And then the king started talking about all sorts of things: about Jonathan and about how he, David, and Jonathan had been the best of friends and how he'd wept when Jonathan was killed and how he hadn't known any of the family was still alive but now he saw Mephibosheth it was like seeing Jonathan again and he wanted to do something for him.

David went on about a promise he'd made and how he was giving Mephibosheth all the land that had belonged to his grandfather. And there was an old servant called Ziba. And

King David was arranging things so that not only Ziba was to be Mephibosheth's servant but all Ziba's family were to work for him, looking after the land he'd been given. And the king also said that he could stay in the royal palace and eat with him at his table. And so it was lucky Mephibosheth had the land to bring in some money, because if you're going to live in a royal palace, you need money. Even if the food comes free, you've still got to buy clothes and things. And pay servants…

One way and another, it was all very confusing. But it wasn't living in a palace that was strange. It wasn't having meals with the king. And it wasn't being rich and having servants that was special. What was strange was the thought that he mattered. That someone not only cared about him but took the trouble to show it.

Much later, Mephibosheth heard from old Ziba how it had all come about. King David had sent for *him* one day, knowing that he'd been one of his grandfather's servants. And the king had asked him if there were any of King Saul's family still alive because he'd made a promise to help them if he could, out of his friendship for Jonathan. And even when Ziba told him that Mephibosheth was disabled King David hadn't backed off or anything. Because some people did in those days – as they still do: they don't want to have anything to do with someone who's different in some way… No, King David sent for him and so here he was – and that was what was important to Mephibosheth: not the money, not living in a palace, but knowing that someone thought he mattered. ◆

7

Esther the Good and Haman the Wicked

Esther was a Jewish heroine who became queen to Xerxes, King of Persia. Because the king favoured her, she was able to save her people from destruction planned by the wicked Haman. The Jewish festival of Purim which occurs one month before Passover (that is, usually about a month before Easter) commemorates her story.

When the Book of Esther is read in synagogues at this festival, children make as much noise as they can every time the villain Haman is mentioned. Besides hissing and stamping their feet, they use football rattles, whistles and even dustbin lids! The aim is to drown Haman's name with noise. Users of this book must decide for themselves whether or not to encourage this custom.

NB Instead of the Persian name Xerxes, the Authorized Version of the Bible uses the Hebrew variant Ahasuerus.

This is a story about good guys and mean guys; guys who get to be important and powerful – and then turn cruel. And it's the story of a beautiful girl called Esther and of a wicked man called ... Haman!!!

◆

IT ALL TOOK place long ago in a country called Persia. In those days, its king was a man some called Xerxes [*say*: **zerk-sees**]. And at that time, there lived in Persia many Jewish people – including Esther. Her parents had both died and she'd been brought up by a cousin, Mordecai, who was much older than she was.

So this is a story about four people:

- King Xerxes
- beautiful Esther
- her cousin Mordecai (who, like Esther, was Jewish)

• and then there was wicked Haman.

It all began when King Xerxes quarrelled with his wife and started looking for a new queen. And as soon as he saw Esther, he knew that she was the one. And that's what happened: Esther became Queen Esther. But on Mordecai's advice, she didn't tell the king that she was a Jew and not a Persian. Just in case, he said, it made him quarrel again.

Now, not long after all this, Mordecai heard of a plot to kill King Xerxes. Mordecai told Esther. She told Xerxes. The king checked it all out. It was true. And he was so pleased with Mordecai that he had his name noted down in all the state papers as 'Official Hero'. Well, time went by until a man we've heard of, a man called, yes, Haman became chief minister. Xerxes told everyone that, in future, they must bow down low whenever they met Haman, to show respect to him.

But Mordecai (who didn't think much of this new chief minister) refused to bow down low to him, as if he was worshipping him. This made the new minister hate Mordecai and think how he might get his own back on him.

In the end, wicked Haman decided to get his revenge not just on Mordecai but on every Jew in Persia. He persuaded King Xerxes that all the Jews in the country should be put to death on a certain day. Mordecai went straight to Esther: 'You must go to the king and beg him not to let this happen. You can't let this happen to your people.'

So Esther thought up a plan and went to the king. 'Please, Your Majesty, my husband, I should like you and your chief minister to come to a banquet I am preparing for you tonight.'

And that's what happened. It was a splendid banquet and the king and the minister were obviously enjoying it. Esther could ☛

see they were both in a splendid mood – so it seemed it might be a good moment to ask a favour. But she decided to be patient. She asked them to come to another even better banquet the next night.

'Delighted,' they both said and each set off for home.

On his way, wicked Haman met Mordecai. Once again, Mordecai refused to bow down to evil Haman. This made the chief minister furious. He arranged to have a tall gallows built on which he could have Mordecai hanged by the neck.

Meanwhile, that same night, the king was unable to get to sleep. He wanted someone to read him a story. And the story he was read was one from the official state papers. It told how, some time back, a man called Mordecai had saved him from a murderous plot. Xerxes had forgotten all about this. He'd even forgotten who Mordecai was but he decided, next morning, to reward him.

So, next morning, when Haman arrived at the palace, ready to ask permission to have Mordecai put to death, the king interrupted him.

'Your Majesty,' began Haman.

'Ah yes,' said the king. 'I've decided to honour a certain man.'

'Would it be me?' smirked the minister.

'No,' said the king.

'Oh.' The minister was crestfallen.

'No,' said the king. 'It's a man called Mordecai.'

'That's all ri— What? You said Mordecai!'

'Yes. Send him my second best royal robes and arrange for him to ride through the city on a royal horse. See it all goes right, won't you?'

The wicked minister was *livid*. But there was nothing he could do about it though. He had to carry out the king's orders.

Well, by now it was evening and time for Esther's second banquet. The king was in a very cheerful mood and asked her if he could grant her a wish in return for the splendid banquets. Her patience had been rewarded.

'Yes,' she said. 'Spare my people, the *Jewish* people, the people who are to be put to death by Haman!'

The king stormed out of the room. He needed time to think. His wife was Jewish, not Persian! And he'd also just found out that his chief minister, whom he'd trusted and relied on, was plotting to kill Mordecai who'd saved his life... The king didn't know what to do. It was all so confusing.

He went back to Esther. 'I've decided...' he said.

'Yes?' said Queen Esther, helpfully.

'I've decided ... I don't know. Yes, I do know. I've decided what shall happen to my chief minister. He shall die on his own gallows! That's what shall happen to Haman. And you Esther, you and Mordecai shall have all his belongings.'

And that's what happened. And ever since, once a year, Jewish people have remembered how God did not allow their people to be destroyed – but how they were saved by the beautiful Queen Esther.

And every year, the story of Esther is read aloud in Jewish synagogues. And during that story, whenever they hear a certain name, they try to drown out that name with boos and jeers and any noise they can make. And that name is the name of wicked old Haman! ◆

8

Purple cloth sold here

This story is included to show that the pioneers of the early Christian church were not all men and also to show how baptism is the 'rite of passage' by which people become Christians.

Philippi is an ancient city in Macedonia, eight miles north-west from the present port of Kavalla, on the northern Greek coast, midway between Thessalonika and the Turkish border. Annexed by the Romans in 168BCE, it was the site of the battle between Mark Antony and, on the other side, Brutus and Cassius in 42BCE. The Christian apostle Paul visited Philippi on his second missionary journey and the first Christian church in Europe was established here.

What makes you want to join a club or gang or society? The people in it? What they do and talk about? And how do you show you've become a member?

This is the story of a rich woman called Lydia. She lived nearly 2000 years ago – a bit after the time of Jesus – in a town called Philippi in what's now the country of Greece. And Philippi was just a few miles inland from the Mediterranean Sea. Greece, of course, is part of Europe, unlike Palestine (where Jesus lived) which is part of Asia.

◆

IT ALL BEGAN one Saturday. The Jewish Sabbath or 'Shabbat', the holy day of the week for Jews. And they were all down by the river, gathered together to pray and talk. 'They' were a group of Jews who'd left their own country, looking for work and they'd settled here in the city of Philippi in a country then called Macedonia, but (like Palestine) a part of the great Roman Empire which stretched right round the Mediterranean Sea.

As was usual in those times, the women sat a little apart from the men and among them was Lydia. As they talked, she little thought how important that day would be...

In those days, most people knew Philippi for one thing. The battle. It had taken place many years ago before all this. Perhaps eighty years before. Mark Antony had led one army. He and the young Caesar, Octavius Caesar that was. On the other side were Brutus and Cassius. They were two of those who had assassinated the great Julius Caesar. Of course, Lydia and her friends didn't take sides in matters like that.

You couldn't in Lydia's business, it didn't pay. You see, she sold purple cloth. The very best – and her customers were important Romans. For purple was the most expensive colour dye. Anyone could make red or blue or yellow dye. And you could make cheap imitation purple cloth by dying blue cloth red.

But the real, genuine purple dye came only from a shell fish, the murex, which could be found on the shores of the Mediterranean – but only if you knew exactly where to look. Which made it rare, and expensive. That's why only the very rich could afford it: senators; royals; emperors. People like that. And Lydia knew where to find it so she made purple cloth, which she sold to important, wealthy people – which made Lydia important and wealthy.

Anyway, I was telling you about that Saturday. As they were talking, a small group of men arrived. Their leader, a little, wiry man, turned out to be called Paul. He came from a place called Tarsus but he'd been living in Jerusalem. There were two others with him. Silas and a young man called Timothy. Paul was the talker though. It seemed he had been a tentmaker. Tents and sailcloth (to make the sails of sailing boats), that sort of thing.

At first Lydia wasn't inclined to pay much attention to him. But what he had to say was … well, special. Something made her listen. He was talking about a man called Jesus. A man from a place called Nazareth. Lydia had never heard of Nazareth or Jesus – but this man Jesus, Paul claimed, was no less than God's son, come to Earth.

Now Lydia wasn't a fool. She was a clever businesswoman and she wasn't easily taken in. As she had so often said, 'You can't fool me. I know when a man's telling the truth.'

But (as she was to explain later) Paul convinced her that he was telling the truth and that her life was 'empty' without Jesus.

'You see,' she said, 'Paul made me see how I'd been too bothered with trivial things. Things that weren't important in the long run. And the more he told me about Jesus, the more I knew that I must follow the teachings of that man.'

Paul said the way to start was by being baptised, being pushed under the surface of a river! Lydia had heard of people being baptised but she'd never thought it was something she'd agree to. 'Letting myself be made an exhibition of, getting my best Sabbath clothes soaking wet, there in the river for all to see, that's not my style. It would be, well, embarrassing.'

That's what she thought at first. But Paul explained the point of being baptised. 'By being submerged in the water and then resurfacing, that's like dying and being born again. An old life ending and a new life beginning. All our wrongdoings can be washed away, and we can start again, helped by the power of Jesus, knowing that his holy spirit will be with us.'

And that's what happened. To the surprise of everyone, Lydia (whom everyone thought, it must be admitted, was just a little bit 'stuck up') went forward. Asked to be baptised. Paul looked at her and said, 'If you believe with all your heart, you may be baptised.'

Lydia said, 'Yes. I believe. I believe that Jesus is the Son of God.' And, there and then, Paul led her down into the river and said, 'I baptise you in the name of God the Father, the Son and the Holy Spirit,' and he lowered her under the water.

As she said afterwards, 'It was when I came up into the sunlight again that I really *knew*. Knew God was with me and that I'd joined the friendship of all believers.'

And what makes that Saturday an important day, there in Philippi, is that Lydia was the very first known person in all of Europe to be baptised a Christian. ◆

9

Pray for Avircius

In the catacombs of Rome (which, in classical times, were not primarily a Christian hiding place but burial chambers) is the tombstone of an early Christian. Part of the inscription reads:

My name is Avircius, a disciple of the pure shepherd who feeds the flocks of sheep on mountains and plains... To Rome he sent me. Everywhere I met with the brethren. With Paul before me I followed, and Faith everywhere led the way...

These things I, Avircius, ordered to be written. I am truly 72 years old... Pray for Avircius.

This story is a fictional account of how he might have become a Christian: it might best be used in conjunction with the previous story.

It shows how some people are prepared to risk everything for what they believe.

NB Early Christians in Rome spoke Greek: it was the language of the Christian church until the third century.

Think of somewhere you really like going. Perhaps the seaside or the local leisure centre. Perhaps the cinema or a theme park or ... [*the reader may suggest specific local attractions*].

Now imagine you could get into really serious trouble if you were seen there. Just suppose there was a chance of being beaten up or even killed, would you still want to go there?

And now suppose there were powerful bullies who wanted to stop you going to church or another place of worship. Would you risk going there? In a time when it was very dangerous to be known to be a Christian, a young man called Avircius [*say:* a-ver-see-us] took that risk – and this is his story. It happened not far from where Lydia sold purple cloth, and not all that long after she became a Christian.

◆

IT WAS A clear blue sky with hardly a cloud to be seen. The sun beat down on the rocky hillside of central Greece. A man and his grown-up son sat watching over their flock of scraggly goats as they grazed on what little grass grew in the stony ground. Far below them, in the distance, you could see the dark green olive groves and the village where they lived. Beyond that, were the calm blue-green waters of the Mediterranean Sea. All that could be heard was the occasional bleat of a goat or the cry of a hawk soaring high above them in the sky.

At last, the older man spoke. 'If you really must talk about such things, it's better to talk up here. Goats don't gossip.'

His son stood up, impatiently. 'Papa, you don't understand. I'm *proud* of what I'm doing. I don't mind if people know.'

His father pulled a piece of grass out of the ground and began to chew it. 'That's daft,' he said. 'What you're talking about is dangerous. You don't seem to realise just how much against it the Romans are.'

'But Papa, it matters to me.'

His father sighed.

'I'm sorry if I'm a disappointment to you.'

'No, Avircius. Not a disappointment. A worry more like.'

The thing was, his father, Daos, was not as poor as some of the villagers. As well as the goats and an olive grove, he owned a fishing boat. So he made quite a good living and, because he knew his son was clever, he had sent him away to school in the city of Athens. And while Avircius was in Athens, and meant to be studying grammar and public speaking, he had met a man ☛

called Paul. Yes, the same Paul who had become a follower of Jesus and the same Paul who had baptised Lydia. Avircius had listened to Paul when he spoke to all the clever men of Athens about Jesus. While Paul didn't convince everyone, he did convince Avircius – and Avircius had decided he must become a Christian, like Paul.

'It's just a whim,' said Daos. 'Just something you think you'll do —'

'No, Papa. It's not like that. I've thought about it. Properly. Father, I've been learning more and more about what they believe.'

But his father had got a point. As more and more people became Christians, the Romans (who, you'll remember, ruled all that part of the world) began to turn against Christianity. There were even stories going around that they were executing people who became Christians.

Avircius thought this most unfair. 'I don't see why they should pick on Christians. They let us ... let *you* worship the Greek gods. And they let the Jews worship how they want.'

But that didn't alter the fact that it had become dangerous to be a Christian. Avircius sat down again, sulking.

'Listen my boy,' said his father, 'we may like to think we can do what we like. But we can't. The Romans rule.' Avircius just grunted. But Daos had more to say.

'You must admit your Christians are a pretty odd bunch. Oh yes, I've heard the stories when I take the fish and olive oil to market. They're always meeting together in secret. Sharing everything they own. Giving away money. They're crazy. Crazy!'

Avircius started to interrupt but his father hadn't finished.

'I tell you, they sound like revolutionaries. And some of them are slaves. You can't blame the Romans for getting tough if their slaves run off to join a secret society. Anyway, you've been well educated: they're not your sort of people.'

'They are, Papa. My sort of people. I've decided I'm going to become a Christian. That's what I want to do with my life.'

His father sighed again. 'You'll have a short enough life if the Romans catch you.'

But Avircius was sure he would be all right. 'I'm going to spread the word of Jesus. I might even go to Rome. Don't worry. I'll survive.'

And years later, he did go to Rome, the very heart of the Roman Empire – and he did survive, at least until he was 72! And we know that because you can still see these words carved on the wall of an underground cellar where those early Christians used to hide:

> My name is Avircius, a disciple of (Jesus) the pure shepherd who feeds the flocks of sheep on mountains and plains... To Rome he sent me. Everywhere I met with the brethren. With Paul before me I followed, and Faith everywhere led the way...

> These things I, Avircius, ordered to be written. I am truly 72 years old... Pray for Avircius. ◆

10

Alban the Martyr

While there is some debate as to whether there ever was such a person as Alban, he is widely regarded as the first English Christian martyr and his story was chronicled in detail by Bede in his History of the English Church and People *(completed in 731CE). Alban's own dates are disputed: Bede places his martyrdom in the year 301. Others give it various dates in the third and fourth centuries.*

Even if it is only a legend, his story is an interesting part of our heritage and a reminder that Christianity in England pre-dates the arrival of Augustine at Canterbury in 597. The story also shows how an individual maintained his beliefs against all odds.

This is a story about a man on the run from soldiers, about a disappearing river and an execution. It happened in England in the days of the Roman Empire, and it's about a man called Alban who gave his name to the city of St Albans (which is about 20 miles north of London).

◆

VERULAMIUM WAS WHAT the Romans called it. It wasn't just a town, it was a city. And an important one at that. It was on the long, straight Roman road known as Watling Street which ran northwards from London. Verulamium was also a garrison. Roman soldiers were always there, ready to make sure everyone kept the laws of the Empire – and strict laws they were too.

One of these laws made it a crime to be a Christian. If a Christian was caught and refused to bow down and worship a statue of one of the old Roman gods, well, that meant the death sentence.

At the time of this story, there were very few Christians in

England: only a few people had heard about Jesus from travellers from other parts of the Empire. But in Verulamium there was one man (whose name we don't know) who *was* a Christian and, what's more, he was a Christian priest. And when the Romans found out about him, he had to escape.

Luckily for him, a man called Alban (who was British but also a Roman citizen) took pity on him and hid him in his house. And while the priest was hiding there, he told Alban about Jesus and Alban became a Christian himself. Which was fine – until someone gossiped about the man hiding in Alban's house and the news reached the Governor of Verulamium. He immediately sent soldiers to search the house but, by the time they got there, Alban had given the priest his own Roman cloak and the priest had got away without being recognised. So the soldiers arrested Alban and took him to the Governor who started questioning him.

'So he was in your house – yes?'

'I gave him shelter. Food, yes.'

'You admit you concealed a Christian priest in your house? You know the punishment?'

Alban said nothing.

'And then you let him escape?'

'I *helped* him escape. I gave him my citizen's cloak that he might have free and safe passage.'

The Governor was furious and started shouting at Alban. 'Since you chose to hide a man who is not only a rebel against the laws of the great Roman Empire but who refuses to worship the divine gods of our Empire and what's more speaks against them —'

He paused to catch his breath – and then started again. 'Since you concealed him from my soldiers, then you will pay the penalty he should have paid for his blasphemy – which you must know is death. Unless... unless you get down on your knees now and beg mercy of me, Governor of this city of Verulamium by the power of the mighty Emperor Diocletian; and say you now worship our god Phoebus, god of the sun.'

But Alban refused to do that. 'I will not offer prayers to your stone statues, to your pagan gods. I follow the way of the true God who promises everlasting life in heaven.'

And it was then that the Governor ordered his soldiers to take Alban, flog him and execute him.

They led him out of the city, down to the bridge which crossed the river and led to the hill where the execution was to take place. But so large were the crowds who came to watch, there was no hope of crossing the bridge. While the soldier in charge of the execution was wondering what to do, Alban prayed they would find a way across the river (because he knew he was certain to be executed and he wanted it to happen as quickly as possible).

And, as he finished praying, the river stopped flowing and the river bed started to dry up. At that, the soldier was so moved he refused to execute Alban. The Governor issued another order.

'Then you'll die as well as him. Now. Both of you.'

'Before I die,' said Alban, 'I should like ... water. A drink.'

At once, a stream of water began to bubble out of the ground. Before anything else could happen, the Governor issued yet another order.

'Right, you over there. In the front rank. Yes, you. Ever beheaded a man? 'Cause you've got two opportunities now. Alban and this clown of a so-called soldier... Use his sword.'

And so Alban was executed, as was the soldier. But people did not forget Alban, the man who'd helped the Christian priest and who'd refused to do or say what he knew was wrong. And many years later, after the Romans had left Britain, a great church was built there in Alban's honour and the city of Verulamium was given a new name: St Albans. ◆

11

St Martin and the beggar

St Martin was born in what is now Hungary about 315CE, and brought up in Italy, the son of an officer in the Roman army. While still a youth, he himself joined the army. Later, after becoming a Christian, he left the army to become a monk. In 371, by popular demand (although reluctant), he became Bishop of Tours in France.

A message of this story is that it requires courage to maintain a course of action which you know to be right but which others mock as being stupid or cowardly.

Can you remember a time you were being laughed at or teased because everyone said you were doing something silly or stupid? Now, it *may* have been something silly, but then again it might not.

If you're doing something that you know is right or good or kind and people laugh at you, it's not easy to stick to what you believe is right. This is the story of a person who was brave enough to keep on doing what he thought was right – even though people made fun of him.

◆

MARTIN WASN'T REALLY a man; not yet. But more than a boy. He was fifteen; strong, fit and quite tall. Tall enough to join the Roman army (because this was in the days when the Romans still ruled most of Europe).

And that was what he was doing now in a small town in Italy, not far from where he lived. Joining the army. The army doctor had examined him and all the other young men who were hoping to become soldiers. Next an officer asked them questions, making sure they were not runaway criminals or slaves who ought to be at home serving their masters.

Each of the young men had brought with him a letter from someone, recommending him as likely to be a good soldier. Martin handed over his letter. The officer read it. 'Most impressive,' he said. 'From your father, isn't it?'

'Yes sir,' said Martin.

'Met him once. In Macedonia. Very brave soldier. And you're going to be just like him. Excellent.'

Martin took the army oath, saying he would be a soldier and be loyal to the Roman Empire and he was given, as was usual, four months pay in advance. The only trouble was he didn't want to be a soldier.

Martin's family worshipped the Roman gods, especially Mars the god of war. And in their home (or villa) in Italy there were statues of Mars – which, of course, was not surprising seeing that Martin's father was a brave and famous army officer (who wanted his son, Martin, to be like him). But Martin had other ideas.

As a young boy, he'd heard about a 'new' religion: people who followed the teaching of a man called Jesus. These people were called Christians. They thought it wrong to go to war, to fight and kill – and Martin thought so too. Secretly, he wanted to become a Christian and to spend his life praying and helping people, but he was obedient and did what his father wanted – which was why he was now a soldier.

In fact, Martin proved to be a very good soldier. He was reliable and popular. Soon, he was promoted. He became an officer: only a junior officer but, still, an officer. Now he wore a sword and a warm red cloak over his armour – and no longer marched on foot with all the other soldiers as they tramped the ☛

long miles along the straight Roman roads. Martin rode on a silver white horse.

The winter when Martin was eighteen, he and his soldiers were posted to another part of the Roman Empire. They were sent to guard the town of Amiens in the north of what's now called France but was then called Gaul. Martin and his soldiers weren't too pleased about this. Winter in northern France can seem very damp and cold to someone used to the warmth of Italy and the sunny Mediterranean countries. But at least Martin had his cloak.

One raw, damp evening, Martin was riding slowly through the town, his soldiers marching behind him, when he saw a beggar. Nothing unusual in that: there were many beggars in those days. But Martin couldn't help noticing this man. He was wearing just a few damp, torn rags and shivering with cold.

Martin pulled up his horse, drew his sword and with one swift movement, cut his warm red cloak in two – and gave half to the beggar who could hardly believe his luck. Martin's soldiers were amazed. They began to giggle. Had their officer gone mad? Ruining his cloak for a beggar? They tried not to laugh out loud. They couldn't help it. But Martin wasn't angry with them. 'That man was cold. I'd got a cloak. It was right to share it.'

In silence, they marched back to their barracks.

That night, Martin had a dream. He thought he saw Jesus, wearing half a Roman soldier's cloak. 'Look,' said Jesus in the dream, 'this is the cloak which Martin has shared.'

His dream made Martin more and more determined to become a Christian and indeed that's what happened. He was baptised and so became a follower of Jesus. Now he wanted to leave the

44

army even more but a war was beginning against a fierce tribe called the Goths. When he tried to leave Martin was immediately accused of being a coward, of wanting to run away from the war. When he still refused to fight, this was thought to be mutiny and so he was put in prison. Only at the end of the war was he released and allowed to leave the army.

He decided then to give up everything. He became a monk, sharing everything with the other monks and helping the poor people of that part of France. He became so popular with the people that, when they needed a new bishop, they insisted that Martin should be their bishop.

Now he could live in a bishop's palace. But no: he shared all his new wealth and lived in a simple wooden hut with his friends, the other monks. And there he taught that we should love one another, help those in need and share what we have. ◆

12

Gerasimus and Jordan

Gerasimus lived in the fifth century and spent most of his life in Palestine and Egypt. About 455CE he founded a 'laura' near Jericho. A laura was a colony of holy hermits who lived in separate huts, spending their time in solitary prayer and meditation, but subject to the rule of an abbot.

The idea of holy people having a special relationship with animals is common in Christianity. Such stories carry two messages: that Christians should respect God's creation, and that they should always be ready to help whoever is in need.

'Doing someone a good turn' may seem quite a little thing – if that person is a friend. But it's not so easy to do someone a good turn if you don't like them – or if you're afraid of them. This is the story of a man who was prepared to give help when it was needed, even though he was afraid. He was called Gerasimus and he lived over 1500 years ago; that is, about 400 years after the time of Jesus. Even when he might have been forgiven for running away, he stayed to give help…

◆

IN THE LAND where Jesus once lived there is a river, the River Jordan. Not far from that river is a city called Jericho and not far from Jericho is a desert. Many, many years ago, on the edge of the desert there lived a number of holy men. Each lived in his own little hut and spent his time praying and thinking about God. They tried to keep themselves away from all the wicked things in the world and some people called them hermits. The proper name for them is 'anchorite'. One of these men was called Gerasimus.

There came a day when Gerasimus decided he would go for a

walk by himself in the desert so that he could concentrate very hard on his thinking. On and on he walked, hardly looking where he was going. Then from behind some rocks, he heard a whimpering noise.

'Oh dear me,' he said. 'I suppose I'd better see what's the matter.'

When he saw what was making the whimpering noise, he said again, 'Oh dear. Oh dear me. You're in pain.'

He was about to go forward and help, but then he stopped as he realised exactly what was in front of him. 'Oh dear,' he said yet again. 'You're a lion. I've never seen one before but I know what you are. I suppose I ought to be afraid.'

The lion whimpered again and held up a paw. And Gerasimus saw that, sticking in the pad of the lion's foot, was a very large and very sharp thorn.

Instead of running away, Gerasimus tip-toed up to the lion and, very gently, pulled out the thorn. Then the lion stood up. Gerasimus started to back away. 'Nice lion,' he said. 'Stay.'

But the lion still came towards him. Gerasimus wondered whether to run or stand still. He decided to turn round and walk slowly away. When he'd gone a few steps, he glanced over his shoulder. The lion was following him. It was so grateful it refused to leave him. It followed him all the way back to where he lived.

At first the other holy men were decidedly frightened but they soon realized that the lion would never hurt a friend of Gerasimus. So the lion came to live with them. Because Gerasimus had found it near the River Jordan, they named it Jordan – and Gerasimus taught it to fetch and carry things for the monks.

☞

Although Jordan was very friendly to all the hermits, his special friend was always Gerasimus. Which might seem like a happy ending but, in fact, the story has a rather sad ending because not all that long after this, Gerasimus died. But *that* wasn't the sad part of it because Gerasimus was an old man by that time, at the end of his life, and he died quietly, without any pain.

No, the sad part of it concerned Jordan, for Jordan was lost without his special friend – and when the other hermits dug a grave and buried Gerasimus's body, Jordan lay down beside the grave and died as well.

This story was written down some years afterwards so people would not forget about Gerasimus who was such a good man that he was later called St Gerasimus. ◆

13

Fire at **Bamburgh**

---

*This story shows how Christianity spread through northern Britain from
Celtic roots and, in particular, from a monastery on the Scottish island of
Iona. One of the monks there, Aidan, was sent to Lindisfarne (Holy
Island) in 635CE in answer to a request from Oswald, King of
Northumbria. He started a monastery on Lindisfarne (which is
connected to the coast of Northumberland by a causeway) where he and
other monks taught local boys Latin and how to make illuminated copies
of the Bible. (The exquisite* Lindisfarne Gospels *survive and are in the
keeping of the British Museum.)*

*Northumbria was only one of the several kingdoms into which
England was then divided. Another, called Mercia, stretched from the
Humber to the Thames and was ruled at this time by King Penda.*

One of the first men to bring the Christian message to the
north of England was a monk called Aidan. He came from
the Scottish island of Iona and made his new home in the
Kingdom of Northumbria, long before Britain was one
united country, in the reign of King Oswald.

◆

IT WAS ALL very satisfactory thought Oswald, as he stood
on the battlements of his fine castle, looking out over the long
white sands of Bamburgh beach. His was indeed a fine castle,
easily defended, perched proudly on an outcrop of rock. Not
that he feared it would be attacked: his kingdom of Northumbria was at peace now, after he had won that last battle.

Yes, everything was fine, thought Oswald. Except that he had
one slight worry in his mind: a promise he'd made and not yet
kept.

The morning before that last battle, he'd made a Christian ☞

cross out of wood, called all his soldiers together and made them kneel before it. Oswald had then prayed aloud, asking God to defend his soldiers and guide them in the fighting. And that was when he'd made his promise, silently – but he'd still made it. It was this: if he could drive the enemy from his kingdom and bring peace to Northumbria, then he would do all he could to teach his people about Jesus and the Christian religion, something they knew nothing about.

As it turned out, his soldiers had little trouble in winning that battle: they soon drove the enemy onto marshy ground where they were easily defeated. Oswald then named the battle area Heavensfield and went back to Bamburgh, where he was now wondering how to keep that promise.

He himself had heard about Christianity when he was a boy and his father had sent him north to Scotland, to an island called Iona where he had been taught by the Christian monks who lived there. And, as he remembered his time at Iona, the answer became obvious. He'd send a messenger there, asking the monks to send one of their number to Northumbria to teach his people.

Which he did. And the monk who came from Iona to Northumbria was called Aidan. Oswald wanted him to live comfortably in Bamburgh Castle but Aidan politely said no.

'I'd like to live on an island like Iona, a place apart where I can be quiet and pray and read. But not so far away I can't reach the mainland and the people of your land.'

'It's lucky,' replied Oswald, 'that I've got such a place. We call it Lindisfarne. You can see it from here. Six miles to the north. Six miles by boat, more if you insist on walking.'

'You can walk to this island?' asked Aidan.

The king laughed. 'Yes. It's only an island at high tide. When the tide goes out, you can walk across the sand to reach it.'

So that was where Aidan settled. Other monks came to join him on Lindisfarne which soon came to be known as Holy Island. They built a church, the first church in Northumberland. They built places for the monks to sleep in and to eat in. They built a guest house, a hospital, and they kept bees. From the bees' wax they made candles and from the honey they made a drink called mead: Lindisfarne Mead, as it's still called. And then they built what Aidan called 'the second most important building' (the first being the church).

And this was the library. For the monks of Lindisfarne were going to busy themselves making copies of the Bible in beautiful handwriting and decorating them in splendid colours.

But Aidan also spent time travelling around Northumbria teaching the people about Jesus – and King Oswald often travelled with him.

All was well in Northumbria. That is, until the fierce army of King Penda, a cruel and pagan king, came north from the land of Mercia, attacking towns and villages and stealing from the people. Oswald locked himself inside his castle.

Outside, close to the south gate, Penda's men were building a huge bonfire. They stole thatch and wood from all the houses round about and set fire to it. Soon the gate house was on fire. Soon the castle itself would be on fire. Soon Oswald would be captured or burned to death.

Across the bay on Lindisfarne, Aidan and another monk called James watched. Then they felt a south wind start to blow, making the fire burn all the more fiercely.

'If only the wind would change,' said James, 'it would save the castle – and the fire would blow back on Penda's men.'

'I think it might be right to pray,' said Aidan. And he did.

'The wind's dropping,' said Brother James.

'It's not!' said Aidan, firmly. 'It's changing direction!' And it was. The fire now blew back towards Penda's men. Soon they were fleeing – and Bamburgh Castle and King Oswald were saved: saved by the prayers of Brother Aidan who nowadays is called St Aidan. ◆

14

England's Nazareth

In the eleventh century, Richeldis de Faverches, lady of the manor of Walsingham in north Norfolk, had a vision in which she was told to build a replica of the home of Jesus in Nazareth. Her 'holy house' was built in 1061CE and within a century became a major Christian shrine. Pilgrims from all over Europe visited it until 1538 when Henry VIII, who had earlier made the pilgrimage himself, ordered its destruction. In 1922 the then parish priest, Alfred Hope Patten, revived the tradition. Pilgrims began visiting Walsingham once again and a new 'holy house' was built in 1931, inside a new shrine church.

Jerusalem, Rome, Canterbury... all famous places. But, once upon a time, a tiny market town in Norfolk in the east of England was just as famous as these. To get there, you have to travel along narrow country lanes and through villages called Little Snoring and Great Snoring. And then you come to Walsingham. But why Walsingham? What's so special about it? Why have thousands and thousands of people gone there over the years? And why is it sometimes called 'England's Nazareth'?

◆

LONG AGO, WHEN Edward the Confessor was King of England (so the story goes), there lived in the tiny market town of Walsingham a rich, important lady called Richeldis.

One day, as she prayed, something strange happened. Although she could hardly believe it, it seemed that Mary, the mother of Jesus was standing there before her.

Mary told Richeldis that she was to have a special house built in Walsingham. It was to be like the one in which Jesus had ☛

grown up in Nazareth. It was to be a place where people could pray, and feel close to Jesus.

At first, Richeldis was not sure what to do. Then Mary appeared to her again, and again. Each time with the same message. Richeldis arranged for builders and carpenters to start work. But where was the house to be built?

As Richeldis considered this, a spring of water suddenly burst out of the ground. It became a well, and there they built the house. People did come to pray and, while they were there, they felt they were in the company of Jesus. People who were ill found that if they drank the water or bathed in it, they were often cured. Walsingham soon became famous, with visitors coming from all over Europe: kings, princes and hundreds of ordinary people. One of the reasons it became so popular was because there were wars taking place in Palestine and so it was dangerous to visit holy places there such as Jerusalem and Nazareth. Instead, people visited 'England's Nazareth'.

Chapels (or little churches) were built along the different routes to the shrine (or 'holy place') where visitors could rest and pray. Only two survive, and one of these is the Slipper Chapel, a mile short of Walsingham. There, the pilgrims would take off their shoes and walk barefoot the rest of the way. Even proud King Henry VIII did this when he visited Walsingham.

But not many years later, in 1538, Henry turned against holy places like Walsingham. The house was pulled down and anything valuable was removed by Henry's men. Over the years, people even forgot where it had been.

But, almost 400 years later, the vicar of Walsingham decided that there should be a new shrine. Arrangements were made to build a new 'holy house'. As the builders started to clear the ground for it, they found an ancient well, packed with clay and, under that, many pairs of shoes which were proved to be several hundred years old! They cleared out the well and it quickly filled up with pure water! Had they chosen the very same spot that Richeldis had been shown 900 years before? Was it the same well that Henry had had blocked up? Well, nobody can say for certain but it's possible!

The new 'holy house' is not meant to be like a real house of the kind that Jesus might have lived in, in Nazareth. Instead, it's meant to be a copy of the house Richeldis built – except that it's built of brick and plaster, and not wood as hers was. A new church was built around it in which services could be held and, since then, hundreds of people have visited Walsingham every year. Some go in the hope of being cured of pain or illness (and many of these people do feel much better for their visit) while others go just to pray and to feel close to Jesus, in England's Nazareth. ◆

15

Murder in Canterbury Cathedral

The story of Thomas Becket is part of our cultural heritage and deserves to be known for that if no other reason. It also usefully makes the point that it can be extremely dangerous to lose one's temper: what is said in an angry outburst cannot always easily be put right.

This is a true story about something that happened in England over 800 years ago. It is the story of a horrible murder which came about entirely as the result of one man losing his temper. In his anger he said something which he later regretted – but by then it was too late...

◆

IT ALL BEGAN with a quarrel. Several quarrels in fact and all of them between the King, King Henry II of England, and Thomas Becket who was Archbishop of Canterbury. Once, they'd been friends: each was the other's very best friend. But sadly they fell out.

At the start of this story, Henry was the most powerful king in Europe. King not just of England but of much of France as well. And Thomas Becket was the grown-up son of a rich merchant. He'd done very well for himself, getting better and better jobs (both in England and Rome) until he got the best job of all. He became Chancellor of England. That meant he was the king's secretary and assistant. Not just doing odd jobs and writing letters for him but being responsible for seeing that everything the king ordered was carried out.

So Becket was powerful. He lived in his own palace which was nearly as luxurious and as well-furnished as the king's. And, as I say, at that time they were good friends.

But Henry had a problem. He was having trouble getting the leaders of the Church, the bishops, to do what he wanted. They didn't like being bossed around by the king. And they felt that not even the king should tell the Church what to do. Henry didn't like that.

Then he had an idea. What he thought was a very good idea. He made his good friend Thomas Becket Archbishop of Canterbury. That meant that Becket would be in charge of all the bishops. Now they would have to do what Becket said. And of course, as Becket was a friend of Henry, that would mean the king would get his own way.

[Whoever was Archbishop of Canterbury was head of the church in England for one good reason. Many years before this, in the year 597CE, a man called Augustine came from Rome to teach the people in southern England about Jesus and the Christian religion. He became the first Archbishop of Canterbury and whoever was archbishop after him was head of the Church of England. But back to King Henry who was hoping his new archbishop, Thomas Becket, would do what he wanted...]

But *that* was not how it turned out. Becket *was* made Archbishop. That happened all right. But he gave up living in luxury and lived as simply as his own priests. What's more, he took the side of the Church. Yes, he tried to be loyal to Henry as well but what mattered most to him now was the Church. Henry felt his old friend had turned against him. And soon they quarrelled. Seriously.

So seriously, Becket had to leave England for his own safety. He went to live in Rome. That was in the year 1164.

Six years later, in 1170, when Becket and Henry were both in France, they met and made up their quarrel. Becket returned ☛

to Canterbury. Everyone treated him as a hero. The people cheered and mobbed him as he made his way into the city. Again Becket became the champion of the Church and soon the king's temper flared up again.

Henry had always been quick to lose his temper and, one December day while he was still in France, he lost it well and truly. He was fuming about Becket! 'Who will free me from this turbulent priest?'

Four of the king's knights heard what the king said. They decided he could mean only one thing. He must want Becket 'out of the way'. As the four of them looked at each other, one silently mimed cutting his throat. The others nodded. And so those knights, Sir William de Tracy, Reginald Fitzurse, Richard le Breton and Hugh de Merville, rode north as fast as they could and took a ship across the Channel. Some people say that Henry realised what had happened and sent messengers after them to stop them. If he did, they failed to catch up with them.

On December 29th the four knights arrived in Canterbury and met Becket. An argument took place and Becket went into the cathedral, to pray at one of the altars there. The priests of the cathedral wanted to bar and lock the doors. Becket said no: the Church of God should not be locked. Then, just as it was getting dark, the knights made *their* way into the cathedral and, there, in a holy part of the cathedral (now known as the Martyrdom), with their great heavy swords, they struck down Becket and then killed him.

Christians all over Europe were horrified when they heard what had happened and soon people started calling him *Saint Thomas à Becket*. And it wasn't long before people started making journeys of pilgrimage to Canterbury, to pray where St Thomas was buried.

In the end, King Henry realised how much he was to blame. He too visited Canterbury, walking barefoot, to show just how sorry he was. But Thomas was dead and nothing could alter that. Henry knew that was the case as he knelt to pray at the grave of the man who'd been his best friend. And the king also realised just how dangerous it can be to lose your temper. What you say when you're angry can't always be put right. ◆

16
Hugh of Lincoln

As part of his penance for his role in the murder of Becket, Henry II founded a 'Charter House' (or Carthusian monastery) in Somerset. Henry chose a French monk, Hugh of Avalon (the youngest son of a noble Burgundian family) to be its prior. As prior and later as Bishop of Lincoln, Hugh proved himself to be that comparative rarity: a brilliant yet likable and sympathetic administrator. This story may be read in two parts: it is a celebration of efficiency, fairness and goodness.
NB Lincoln diocese then stretched from the Thames to the Humber.

Eight hundred years ago, the city of Lincoln was one of the biggest in the land. Not so big as it is now, but for those days ... well, a great city.

And 800 years ago, as now, high upon Lincoln Hill, there stood the cathedral – except that then, in the year 1186, it was in ruins. The roof and other parts had come crashing down during an earthquake the year before. And something else was wrong at Lincoln. There was no bishop; no man to be in charge of all the churches and priests in the area all around. This story is about the man who got that job: a man who was good at getting things done.

———————————— ◆ ————————————

BUT OUR STORY doesn't begin in Lincoln or even in the year 1186. It begins 40 years before that, in part of what's now called France. There, in the castle of Avalon, there lived a knight. Yes, a real knight in shining armour! He had three sons: Peter, William, and Hugh.

When their father was at home, Peter and William had him teach them how to fight. But Hugh was different yet, in his own way, just as brave. You see, his mother looked after people who were ill or deformed and also people who suffered from the disease of leprosy. Most folk wouldn't go anywhere near them but Hugh's mother did – and young Hugh had the courage to go and hold the towels while she washed their sores and their damaged hands and feet.

Peter and William grew up to become brave knights, like their father. Hugh decided he would become a monk. That is, he would never marry but spend his whole life praying and studying, with other monks, in a building called a monastery; in fact, a particular kind of monastery called a Charter House.

Hugh loved this peaceful, quiet life and, as the years went by, he became one of the older and most respected monks. A holy man; kind and gentle.

Meanwhile, in England, the king, King Henry II had a problem. [The Archbishop of Canterbury, Thomas à Becket, had been murdered and many people thought it was the king's fault. To prove his sorrow, he'd done various things – and one of them was this:] He'd arranged for a monastery to be built at a place called Witham in Somerset and now he needed a monk to be in charge. He'd heard about quiet, gentle Hugh of Avalon and decided that he needed Hugh. So he sent for him.

Gentle Hugh came to Witham. And what did he find? Just a few huts; nothing else. He got back on his horse and rode straight off to see the King.

'My dear King,' he said as politely as he could, 'do you call that a monastery? A few huts made out of branches? No church! And what about the people who were living on the land before? What's happened to them? No, please don't interrupt —' (Yes, Hugh spoke to the King like that – but he did say 'please') '— I'll tell you what you'll do. You'll give them land to farm and new homes to live in. And you must pay stonema- ☛

sons and carpenters to build a proper monastery. And then —' (he added tactfully) '— everyone will know how generous you are. But if you don't, well, I won't stay in England. Yes?' And he stood there smiling.

'I'll pay,' said the king, with a sigh.

'To the last penny, if you please!' said Hugh, charmingly but firmly – and off he went, back to Witham.

Everyone was very surprised, not least the king. Was this the same, quiet Hugh of Avalon that they'd heard about? But in the end, the monastery was built and Henry realised that Hugh was nowhere near as soft as some people had said. So later, when Henry had another problem, again he thought of Hugh.

This time the problem was Lincoln. For years, Lincoln cathedral had not had a bishop – and it needed one badly. So the king sent a message to Hugh telling him he was now Bishop of Lincoln; he'd be in charge of the Church through nine counties (which meant he'd become one of the most powerful men in the country).

'But I'm happy being a monk,' he said. 'I don't want to go to Lincoln.' In the end though, he agreed and, about 800 years ago, Hugh of Avalon became Bishop of Lincoln. When he got there of course he found his cathedral was in ruins.

He wasted no time. Straight away he arranged for it to be rebuilt. 'It must be bigger. It's God's house and the bigger it is and the more beautiful it is, the more it'll remind the people that there's nothing more important in life than God.'

Bishop Hugh got everyone organised. Stone was quarried and brought to Lincoln. Stonemasons were found to cut and chisel the stones. Carpenters carved the woodwork. Other men made beautiful stained glass windows and the silversmiths got to work. And Hugh kept them all busy. Indeed, that was one of the things he was best at: organising people. And when he could, he joined in himself, carrying wood and stone up to where it was needed. Yes, the most important man in the Church doing one of the most ordinary jobs. It was a little, well, embarrassing. But it made everyone work all the harder!

While he was Bishop of Lincoln, Hugh lived near a place called Stow, not far from Lincoln. Round his house at Stow, there was a moat and, on the moat there lived a fierce swan. When Hugh arrived, his servants warned him about it. 'Leave the door ajar,' he said. 'P'raps it'll come in and see me.'

'It really *is* fierce, please my Lord,' they all said.

But they left the door open and ... yes, in walked the swan. Hugh held out a piece of bread. With a little flap of its wings, it stretched out its neck and took the bread. From then on, Hugh and the swan became friends. But Hugh often had to travel away from Stow. And the swan *always* seemed to know when he was coming back.

Just before he arrived, it would get terribly excited and swim up and down, making an enormous fuss. And then when Hugh came through the gate, it would come quietly up to him. He began to hide bread for it up his sleeve, and the swan would push its beak gently up the sleeve looking for the bread.

Meanwhile, the rebuilding of Lincoln cathedral went on. And Hugh was also busy building hospitals and helping anyone in trouble – like the time he was in a town called Stamford. A group of Jewish people who lived there had been accused of breaking the law even though they were quite innocent. Bishop Hugh saw that a crowd of people were attacking them ☛

with sticks and stones. Without hesitating, he strode straight into the middle of the riot. He spoke firmly to them all. He calmed them down, even made a few jokes (which made them laugh and lose their anger). Then he made sure everyone was treated fairly.

Each autumn, Hugh went back to the monastery at Witham to spend some time in peace and quiet with the monks who still lived there. Even though he was one of the most important men in the country and there were people prepared to do all his jobs for him, he did all his own cooking. And there was something else that he really loved doing. After every meal, he did the washing up. Yes, the bishop insisted on washing up not only his own pots but everyone else's as well. He really did love washing up.

Then came another time, when Hugh was away from Stow. Everyone noticed that the swan had suddenly become very sad. Its wings floated limply in the water, its head drooped.

'Perhaps it's dying,' the people said.

It wasn't though. But as they found out later, just at that moment, far away in London, *Hugh* was dying.

His body was brought back to Lincoln cathedral and thousands of people (including the Kings of England and Scotland) came to his funeral, not to be sad or sorrowful but to give thanks for the man who had given Lincoln such a wonderful building in which to worship God; a man who had done so much to help the sick and to see that ordinary people were treated fairly; a man who'd been so ready to do ordinary jobs himself: strong and gentle Hugh; clever, kind, fierce but friendly, Bishop Hugh of Lincoln. A man who got things done. ◆

17

Francis of Assisi

Francis was born in 1182. The turning point of his life was in 1206 when he left his family and travelled with eleven followers to Rome. In 1215, the Pope allowed him to set up a new order of monks (properly called friars). Franciscan friars give up all personal possessions and live very simply. (Francis was inspired to start his order by reading Matthew, chapter 10, verses 7–20.) An early environmentalist, he taught that we should love and care for all of God's creation. He died in 1226. Two years later he was made a saint.

One of the kindest and most loved Christians of all time must be a man we know as St Francis. He is especially famous for the way he cared for all animals and other living things. But he wasn't just a meek and mild sort of man. Once, when he was in front of a very important churchman (called a bishop), he tore off all his clothes.

Francis was born in the town of Assisi in northern Italy, and he was the son of a rich tradesman, Peter Bernardone [*say*: ber-nar-doe-neh]. As a young man, he gave away everything he owned and tried to live as Jesus had done.

◆

PETER BERNARDONE WAS furious. Really fuming with anger. It was all to do with his boy, Francis (who was really no longer a boy but a young man).

Peter Bernardone (who was very rich) wanted young Francis to enjoy the same sort of life as the other wealthy young noblemen of the town. That way, he thought, his family would be respected and feared by the ordinary people.

At first, Francis had enjoyed going to smart parties and spend- ☞

ing money. His father was satisfied. But then, Francis was ill for a while. As he got better, he started to spend more time on his own, praying. Whenever he could, he gave his money and food to people who were poor and needy. He no longer wore his fine, expensive clothes.

One day, he was praying in a church called St Damian's, just outside Assisi. The church was rather old and almost in ruins. As Francis prayed in front of a large crucifix (which is a cross with a statue of Jesus on it), the statue seemed to speak: 'Francis, repair my church.'

Now, at that time, Peter Bernardone was away on business. So Francis went back home, took some of his father's goods and sold them. Then he took the money to the priest at St Damian's, to pay for the repairs. And that was why Peter Bernardone came to be so furious. As soon as he returned home and found out what had happened, he took his son to see the bishop and told him the whole story.

The bishop listened. Then, turning to Francis, he said gently, 'Francis, the Church cannot take what does not belong to it. You must give back to your father what is his.'

So Francis took the money and gave it back to his father. Then he started tearing off his clothes and throwing them at him. 'Now I owe you nothing, Father! I've got nothing of yours,' he said, taking off the very last of them. 'You're no longer my father and I've no father but my Father in Heaven.'

Peter Bernardone took his money and stormed out. Someone put an old workman's tunic around Francis. His new life had begun. And from that day, Francis lived very simply, owning nothing and eating only the food he could beg. Others joined him and they became known as Franciscans. Among other things, Francis became famous for his love for animals and birds.

This became clear when Francis was outdoors one day, teaching a group of people about God.

'What God wants us to do is —' said Francis.

'We can't hear you!' interrupted the people.

It was true. They couldn't. There was Francis, standing on a little hill, talking to the people. And the reason they couldn't hear him was because a large number of swallows were building nests nearby and chirping very loudly.

'My dear sister swallows,' said Francis. 'Listen to the word of God and be quiet until I've finished.'

To everyone's amazement, the swallows all settled on the edges of buildings and in trees, and were silent.

'Thank you,' said Francis. 'As I was saying, what God wants us to do is to love each other. Be kind to each other. We are all brothers and sisters – even the animals and birds. That is why I call the swallows "sisters"...'

And the swallows kept silent until he had finished teaching. Then, once again, they began to sing.

One winter, many years later, Francis stayed with three or four of his followers, or 'Franciscans', who were like monks but who are known as friars. These friars lived in a cave at a place called Grecchio, near the ancient city of Rieti in central Italy.

Just before Christmas, Francis decided to show the people who lived round about Grecchio just what it had been like for Jesus to be born in a stable. 'Brother John,' he said to one of the older friars. 'I want to talk to you about Christmas.'

'Why, you are going to spend it with us, aren't you? Here at ☛

Grecchio?' asked the old man, afraid that Francis might be leaving them.

'Yes, yes. Yes, I shall spend Christmas here,' said Francis. 'This is a good place.'

It was, too. High up in the mountains, sheltered by the trees that grew on the hillside.

'I've been thinking, Brother John, about the very first Christmas. I want all the people from the villages down in the valley to understand what it was like. John, I want you to arrange something for me.'

Together they made a plan. On Christmas Eve, Francis asked all the people to come to Grecchio, bringing a lighted torch or candle. From all along the valley they came, wondering what they would see. They soon found out. There, at the entrance to the cave, Brother John had placed a manger – the kind of wooden trough which holds hay for animals to eat. Beside it were a man and a woman, looking into the manger where a little bundle of clothes represented a baby. There were other men there, dressed up as shepherds, and a real ox and an ass.

'But that's just how it must have been in Bethlehem,' the people said. 'When Jesus was born.'

Francis was pleased. 'Yes. He was born in a simple stable among brother and sister animals. Let's sing and give thanks to God for sending Jesus to us that very first Christmas.'

And that is what Christians have done at Christmas ever since. ◆

18

Everything's going to be all right

Julian of Norwich was born in 1342 and died (we deduce) well into the fifteenth century at a considerable age. On 8 May 1373, during a sudden and severe illness, she received a series of sixteen 'revelations'. She became an anchoress (see story 12, Gerasimus and Jordan), living permanently alone in a cell attached to St Julian's Church in Norwich. She almost certainly took the name by which we know her from that church. For 20 years, she meditated on the visions she had been granted and recorded them in The Revelations of Divine Love, *the first book to be written by a woman in English.*

Some assembly leaders may feel this is an appropriate story to use at a time when a class is affected by depressing national or international news.

Sometimes, when we watch the news on television, it can all seem very gloomy and sad. There may be a war in one country, a shortage of food in another. There may have been a terrible accident or fighting and killings. People may have done cruel or wicked things. Everything seems to be going wrong.

One person taught us not to get too depressed by the news; never to give up hope. We don't know her name and we know very little about her – except that she wrote a book. But because she lived in a church called St Julian's in Norwich, we call her Julian of Norwich or (sometimes) the Lady Julian. This is her story.

◆

EVERYTHING WAS GOING wrong. First there had been the plague, a terrible illness which had swept across most of Europe, killing thousands of people. Some people called it the Black Death; most hardly dared speak of it. They just mouthed the words by which everyone knew it: 'the Death'. ☞

The first outbreak had happened in Britain at the end of the year 1348. It happened again 20 years later. It was worst in the towns and cities because there people lived close together; the streets were narrow and filthy and without proper drains. No wonder infection spread quickly.

In the city of Norwich (where 30,000 people then lived) it killed at least one person in three, perhaps one in two. That is, at least 10,000 people died. In fact, so many died there weren't enough people left to bury the bodies.

And when the plague was over, there weren't enough men left to plough the fields; there weren't enough men to gather in the crops. So food became scarce – and expensive. The poorest people suffered the most.

And as if all this wasn't bad enough news, England was at war – fighting the French. Then, in 1372, Spain joined in with France against England. There was a huge sea battle – and the English were defeated. Many English sailors were taken prisoner and an English treasure ship was sunk. Back home, there was another poor harvest. It was a miserable winter.

But then came spring and Easter. Would everything get better?

No. Certainly not for one woman who lived in Norwich. A fortnight after Easter, this woman was taken ill. She quickly got much worse and by Wednesday evening everyone thought she was going to die.

Then, early the next Sunday morning, her parish priest visited her, bringing a crucifix, a cross with a small statue of Jesus on it. 'Look at it,' he said. 'Be strong.' At first, she was too weak to move even her eyes. Then she managed to look at the figure of Jesus on the cross. For a moment, the room seemed to go dark and she thought she really was at the moment of her death

– but then she was no longer in pain! During the next twelve hours or so, she saw many wonderful things, in her mind – but very clearly as if they were quite real.

The Lady Julian (which is the name by which we now know this person) got better. Later, she wrote down the many things that she had seen. She was, in fact, the first woman to write a book in English and in it she teaches us what she herself learned.

Just one of many sights that came to Julian was what she called 'a little thing, the size of a hazelnut and round, like a ball'. It was on the palm of her hand. She looked at it and wondered.

'What is it?'

Then an answer came to her. 'It is everything that has been made and everything that will be made.'

It was so small, so fragile, she wondered how it did not break into pieces.

More words came to her.

'It exists because God loves it.'

And from the sight of that 'little thing' (we know no more about it), Julian understood three things:

- God has made everything
- God loves everything
- God looks after everything.

Julian felt that God was telling her that, yes, things do go wrong in the world. People do bad things. It can't be helped. That is the way the world must be – but (because God loves us) in the end, it is all going to be all right. Everything is going to be all right. As she wrote in her book, 'In those words, I saw ☛

one of God's great secrets. And when we share that secret, we shall understand why he had to allow bad things in the world. Until then, we must remember, everything's going to be all right.'

Or as her words are sometimes written, 'All shall be well and all manner of things shall be well.' ◆

19

Mad Margery

Margery Kempe (born about 1373) deserves to be more widely known. She was the daughter of the Mayor of King's Lynn (then called Bishop's Lynn). She became highly (even excessively) religious. Her book, The Book of Margery Kempe *(which she dictated, being illiterate), is a narrative of her life and pilgrimages to Italy, Jerusalem, Spain and Germany – in which she flouted convention by travelling alone (when married women were supposed to be accompanied by their husbands) and by wearing virginal white despite having mothered fourteen children.*

Snobbish and proud in her early years, she experienced severe post-natal depression and a profound religious conversion. Her subsequent enthusiasm and religious ecstasies were a trial to her husband and to those around her. She was given to copious weeping at moments of extreme joy and devotion. But her story is one of conviction, determination and an inspiring refusal to be defeated by teasing.

Her autobiography is one of the earliest books by a woman and the earliest known autobiography written in the English language. For many years, it was 'lost'. Only some of the more devout passages survived in Cambridge University Library. Then the complete book was rediscovered in 1934.

People said she was mad. She didn't mind. She didn't give in when people teased her. She kept to what she believed; she kept to what she thought was right. Her name was Margery Kempe and she lived in King's Lynn (then known as Bishop's Lynn) around the year 1400. That is, about 600 years ago. And she was certainly 'different' – as we shall find out…

◆

MARGERY WAS THE daughter of the town's mayor – and he was a wealthy man. She enjoyed being rich and being thought an important person in the town. And then she mar- ☛

ried John Kempe, who was also quite well off. After they married, she had fourteen children!

In those days, women were expected just to look after their families but Margery Kempe was different. She also ran a brewery which the family owned, where they made the beer that was drunk in the town. And she continued to show off in fine clothes when she went out.

That is, until one night when she was in bed, she thought she heard such sweet music it must be coming from heaven. It changed her life. From then on, she gave up her fine clothes, said sorry for all the things she'd done wrong and set out to serve God. That is, she went to church – often, several times a day. She and her husband went on journeys to holy places such as Canterbury and York. [She also went to Norwich to visit the Lady Julian.] And, most strange of all, she often burst into tears while she was praying or if anything reminded her of how Jesus had suffered on the cross.

She admitted that her weeping and wailing were noisy and violent. 'Boisterous' was the word she used. Sometimes she tried to hold back the noise until she was blue in the face – and then it would burst out, no matter where she was.

But the biggest adventure of her life was when she decided she would travel right across Europe to Jerusalem to see where Jesus had lived and died. She'd be like a medieval hitchhiker, getting what help she could find.

Now, in those times, respectable women did not leave their husbands to go off travelling on their own. But that didn't stop Margery. She set about persuading John to let her go without him – and in the end he agreed.

She travelled first to Yarmouth and from there went by ship

across the sea. She had a lot of trouble on the ship because other passengers made fun of her for saying her prayers and for her weeping. She didn't let that stop her. She still said her prayers, whatever the others said about her.

And then came the long journey, much of it on foot, some of it riding on a donkey, south across Europe. For safety against robbers, she travelled with other Christians who were going to Jerusalem – and again she was teased.

Sometimes they wouldn't let her eat with them. Once they cut her dress short so her legs showed (which women never let happen in those times). Another time, they stole her sheets. Several times they left a place secretly, without her. Then she had either to risk travelling completely alone or wait until she found another group with whom she could travel.

But Margery put up with it all. She was determined to get to Jerusalem, which she did. She saw where Jesus had died on the cross and where he had been buried. She went to Bethlehem where he was born – and in each place she said her prayers and, yes, she cried and cried!

After she got home, she went off on other journeys to other places and when she was much older, she wrote the story of all her adventures in a book. Or, rather, because she'd never learned to write, she told it to two men and they wrote it down for her. This story of her life, her autobiography, is the first autobiography anyone wrote in English – and she was also one of the first women to write a book in English.

So was she a bit mad? Yes, plenty of people said so. But what was special about Margery was that she didn't mind what people said. They were only words. She knew what she believed about Jesus and God, and she believed it was true. She wasn't going to give that up, just because of a bit of teasing. ◆

20

Voices

Joan of Arc (or Jeanne d'Arc, also known as 'the Maid') was born in Domrémy in the Lorraine about 1412CE and was to become France's greatest heroine. She said at first that the voices she heard came in a blaze of light – although later she claimed to have heard them when the church bells rang. Her 'voices' told her to deliver France from the English who were occupying parts of the country.

She inspired the French army to recapture Orléans in 1429 and persuaded the Dauphin, Charles, to be crowned. But the French were divided among themselves, and in 1430 she was captured by the faction fighting for the Duke of Burgundy, who was opposed to the French king. The Burgundians sold her to their English allies and she was burned at the stake as a witch in Rouen on 31 May 1431. She was made a saint in 1920.

NB 'Dauphin' was the title given to the eldest son of the King of France: Charles had succeeded his late father in 1422 but had not been crowned then.

To the French, she is still the great heroine of France. The English said she was a witch. The French called her *Jeanne la Poucelle* (Joan the Maid); the English called her Joan of Arc. Her story began in the year 1425, when England and France were at war – and England ruled part of France.

◆

JOAN WAS AN ordinary country girl, about thirteen years old. But after one summer's day she would never be ordinary again.

She was in the garden, when she heard the voices. They seemed to come from a blaze of light. At first she was frightened, but then she became convinced they were the voices of angels. One was the archangel, Michael. He seemed to be saying she must become a soldier and help the young king of France win the war against the English.

But how could a farmer's daughter do anything like that? So she did nothing. Perhaps the voices would stop. But they didn't. She told her family and friends about them. They were amazed. Some believed her: most didn't. But she became more and more convinced of what she must do.

She left home and went to see the local nobleman. 'I'm called Joan,' she told him. 'I come from the village of Domrémy and I've been told to save France from the English, so please will you give me a suit of armour, a horse and help me get to the king?'

'Why on earth should I believe you?' he asked.

'Because our army is about to be defeated again.'

A few minutes later, news came of that defeat.

The nobleman sent her to the king. He believed her story and sent her on to the commander of the army, a man called Dubois.

At that time, part of the French army was trapped in the city of Orléans. The English army was surrounding the city on three sides. On the fourth side was a river. So how could the French soldiers be rescued from the city?

'Simple,' said Joan. 'We get boats and cross the river and save them.'

'I've got the boats,' said Dubois. 'But the wind's blowing the wrong way. See? They can't get across.'

'Is that all? We just need the wind to change direction?' asked Joan. 'I'll go to church and pray about it.'

When she got back, the wind had indeed changed. The boats ☛

crossed the river, and the two parts of the French army were able to link up and save Orléans.

Under her leadership, the French had many victories against the English, but the English army still occupied part of France. What's more, some of the French were becoming jealous of *la poucelle* – including the Duke of Burgundy (who was actually on the side of the English). Eventually, he managed to capture her and sell her to the English.

They decided that Joan should be put on trial and her judge was to be Bishop Pierre Cauchon. He was French, but on the side of the English (like the Duke of Burgundy). He was a cold man, bad-tempered and full of envy and hatred.

Because Joan had helped the French army to be so successful, the English said that it must mean she was a witch and that she was on the side of the devil. The punishment for this was death by burning. She never stood a chance for the truth was, Bishop Cauchon and the English had agreed secretly before the trial that even if she was found innocent, she would be taken to England and executed.

The trial lasted many, many days. Joan firmly refused to answer what she thought were their silly questions. She told one official she'd pull his ears if he made a mistake in what he said. And she told Bishop Cauchon he'd be in great danger if he judged her wrongly. But still the questions came.

'Whose were these voices?' 'Were they not devil voices?' 'How do you know?'

Then they tried to persuade her that she had been wrong and that the voices had tricked her. For a moment, she thought that if she said she had been wrong she might be set free. Yes, she would agree with them! But, almost at once, she realized this would not mean freedom. They would never set her free! So she went back to her original story – which she believed really was the truth.

'They *were* the voices of the saints,' she said again.

'Guilty,' they all said.

English soldiers took her to the crowded market-place, there in the French town of Rouen. She was taken up on to a platform and tied to a post. Wood was piled up round her feet. An English soldier made her a cross out of two pieces of wood. She asked him to hold it up so she could see it. They set light to the fire. The flames flickered and then burned strongly.

One of those watching was the English king's secretary, a man called John Tessart. As she died, he said: 'We've burned a saint.' But it was not for nearly 500 years that the ordinary village girl from Domrémy did officially become St Joan of Arc. ◆

21

Not easy

This story of Thomas More makes the point that telling the truth is not always easy – but there have been people of principle for whom 'the truth' is worth even the ultimate sacrifice. At a more mundane level, it may teach the point that telling the truth can be more important than popularity or 'safety'.

Until 1534, the Pope was head of the whole Catholic Church which of course included the Church in England. In that year, the Act of Supremacy was passed by Parliament (as is described in the story). Thomas More's opposition to the Act led to his imprisonment, and eventually to his execution in 1535. He was canonized in 1935.

Which is more important: telling the truth or saying what people want you to say? And would you go on telling what you knew to be the truth if it was going to get you into trouble? Some people have had the courage to go on saying what they believe is true, even if it cost them their lives.

In the time of King Henry VIII of England, in a house near the River Thames in London, there lived a man called Thomas More. He was a very clever man: no wonder the King had made him Lord Chancellor of England [just as another king, years before, had made Thomas Becket *his* Lord Chancellor]. But now Thomas was in trouble.

◆

'BUT IT'S EASY. You just say what he wants you to say.' Margaret, a young woman in her twenties, looked pleadingly at her father, Thomas More.

'Margaret, my dear, it's not easy,' he replied.

Thomas More had been a writer and a lawyer. He'd been a Member of Parliament and a judge. He was famous for being wise – so King Henry had chosen him as one of his advisers. And then he'd made him Lord Chancellor. Thomas was rich, powerful and popular. But now, although he was still famous, he was no longer Lord Chancellor. And there was every chance he would be sent to prison, in the Tower of London. Even worse, he might be executed – just because he would not say a few words to please the King. So how had this all come about?

King Henry very much wanted to have a son who would be king when he died. He had a daughter called Mary but no sons – and now the doctors said his wife, Queen Catherine, could not have any more children. So Henry claimed that he had never been properly married to her and he divorced her, just because she would not be able to have any more children.

Henry then married another woman called Anne Boleyn. The Pope, who (in those days) was the head of the whole church and who lived in Rome, said this was wrong. And so, too, did Thomas More. He resigned from his job as Lord Chancellor, in protest and because he felt he could no longer be the king's chief adviser if he believed that what the king was doing was wrong. He also refused to go to the coronation where Anne was crowned queen. All this made Henry very angry with Thomas. But Thomas remained popular with the ordinary people.

Two years later, there was still a lot of gossip about whether Anne Boleyn was truly and legally Henry's wife. So Henry persuaded Parliament to make a law saying that, in England, he himself and not the Pope was head of the church, and that Anne was his legal wife and that her children (and not his daughter Mary) should rule after him. What was more, Henry wanted all the important people in the country to swear by the Holy Bible that all this was true and right. So of course Thomas was asked to swear this holy oath. If he didn't, well, ☞

the king would punish him in some way or other – and the king could do more or less what he liked. Which was why Margaret was now trying to persuade her father to say the oath.

'It's easy,' she said to her father. 'It's just a few words. Say anything if it'll save you.'

'But it's very wrong to say what's not true is true,' her father insisted.

Nothing she could say would persuade him to take the oath. He was put in prison, locked up in a cold, dark, damp cell in the Tower of London. Friends came to see him. They too tried to get him to change his mind: 'If you swear the oath, you can go free.' Thomas kept silent.

'King Henry's getting very impatient,' they told him. He still kept silent.

A year after being put in prison, Thomas was charged with being a traitor to the king and the country: what's called 'treason'. The punishment for treason was execution.

He still refused to take the oath. He was taken to court and found guilty. Later he was beheaded. His head was stuck on a post on London Bridge.

He could have saved himself. He didn't. He kept true to his conscience. It wasn't easy. ◆

22

The journey

*John Bunyan (1628–88) was imprisoned from 1660 for preaching
without a licence. Released in 1672, he became pastor of a church in
Bedford but was again imprisoned for a period during which he wrote
the first part of* Pilgrim's Progress. *A classic of Christian literature, it
takes the form of a dream in which Christian (on the advice of
Evangelist) flees from the City of Destruction and eventually reaches the
Celestial City.*

This story is very loosely based on Pilgrim's Progress *and may serve as
an introduction to that allegory (the style of which is surprisingly direct).
Note that even very young children are familiar with allegorical
characterization (as in the* Mister Men *books). In order to widen the
story's relevance (since the concept of 'life as a journey' is common to
many faiths), Christian and Evangelist have here been renamed Adam
and Conscience. In some situations, it may be appropriate to revert to the
original names.*

This story is a parable, a story with a meaning. With lots of
meanings, in fact. It's about a journey – but not just a
journey from one place to another. This journey is like our
journey through life, as we grow up and learn new things.
On our journey, we meet all sorts of people, problems and
even dangers. We're tempted to do wrong or selfish things –
and all these things happen in this story to a person called
Adam, on *his* journey.

◆

ADAM HATED LIVING in the city. Especially in the summer when the fumes of the traffic smelt the worst. And he
hated the crowds and the rush and the noise. Especially the
noise.

He'd no job. He'd nothing to do all day, except hang around ☞

town – humping a great rucksack on his back. Yes, Adam's rucksack. He just couldn't get rid of it and it was crammed full with worries. Private worries, like those that go on in your head when you've nothing else to think about.

'So what are you going to about it all?' asked Conscience. Conscience was a voice, in Adam's head, who sometimes talked to Adam. Adam knew his Conscience was a good friend but even so he didn't always pay much attention to him.

'It's all very well you saying "do something" but what *can* I do?' thought Adam.

Conscience never needed Adam to speak out loud to know what he was thinking so he answered at once.

'Go somewhere. You're always saying you want to get away from here.'

'So where can I go?'

'I know just the place,' replied Conscience. 'It's a place where there are no problems, no suffering, no pain. It's called Paradise.'

'Oh yeah?' thought Adam.

'Yeah!' said Conscience.

So that was how Adam came to leave the city. He just walked away from the grime and the filth, and set out – straight ahead along the main road. With his rucksack.

The only trouble was, he was so happy at first that he didn't look where he was going. And that is how he came to fall into a slimy, filthy patch of mud called Misery Marsh. It was deep. Seriously deep. Adam felt himself sinking. He struggled and struggled, determined to get himself out of it. At last, as he was almost being sucked under, he called out, 'Help!'

And immediately he felt someone pulling him out of the marsh. 'Who are you?' he asked in surprise, as he reached dry ground.

'My name's Help,' said Help. 'I'm usually around, ready to help, just as soon as anyone asks.'

'But you waited till I asked,' said Adam, almost angrily.

'I never interfere,' said Help. 'I just help when I'm asked.'

'And you mean there are people who never ask for help?'

'Yes,' said Help. 'Amazing, isn't it?'

Adam met many other people on his journey. He met Mr Know-It-All who advised him not to follow the main road but to take a side-track. Adam gave in to the temptation and soon found that it just went round in circles, leading nowhere. As Conscience pointed out, Adam was easily side-tracked.

And then Adam came to the Interpreter's house. She explained things to Adam. She helped him wash off all the mud of Misery Marsh and she also told him he could leave his rucksack of worries there. As she said, 'There's no point hoarding worries. Share them with a friend: that's what friends are for.'

What's more, she gave him a book which would guide him on the rest of his journey. It was to be a journey that would take him through the frightening and spooky Valley of Shadows (but the book told him not to be afraid). Next, he made a good new friend called Faith. The journey was much easier while he travelled with her – that is until he lost her at a fun-fair called Vanity Fair. Here he was tempted to try to win a fortune and then he wasted ages admiring himself in a hall of mirrors. Next he went on the dodgem cars (which were all one-seater cars as no-one ever shared anything at Vanity Fair) and so it was a ☛

long time before Conscience could persuade him to leave such things behind and to continue on his way.

Luckily, he soon made another new friend called Hopeful who encouraged him when he was tired and weary with his travelling. And when Adam got lost again, Conscience had to remind him that he'd got a book which would show him the way. No sooner did he start to read it again, than he once more found Faith.

Even so, it was a long, long journey and Adam often wondered why he had to make it. Except that, despite all the problems, lots of it was really quite enjoyable and, as he went along and got older and wiser, he began to understand just how pleasant it would be when he got to Paradise.

Which, in the end, he did – by keeping to the Straight and Narrow Path. But he only got there thanks to the book he had been given, and also thanks to the help of three good friends: Faith, Hopeful and his very best friend, Conscience. ◆

23

Something must be done

Elizabeth Fry (1780–1845) was a member of the Society of Friends (or Quakers) who became famous for her prison reform work. She was born Elizabeth Gurney and had six sisters and four brothers. Unusually for Quaker families of that time, the Gurneys did not live the life of 'Plain Quakers', wearing dark, plain clothes and believing music and dancing were wicked. In the language of the period, they were 'wide'.

Elizabeth was a courageous, indomitable woman who achieved a great deal in what was very much a male-dominated society. The tragedy is that the reforms she achieved did not all survive her.

You've probably seen pictures on television from inside a prison: the landings, the little rooms or cells in which prisoners are locked up. Two hundred years ago, prisons were even more horrible places, as we're going to hear.

But one person thought something should be done about them – and her married name was Elizabeth Fry. She was a Christian and a member of a group of Christians who are called the Society of Friends. They are often known simply as 'Friends' or 'Quakers'.

◆

WHEN SHE MARRIED, Elizabeth and her new husband, Joseph, moved to London. In the next 22 years, they had eleven children. Elizabeth Fry, who now wore the plain, dark dresses and white head-dress worn by most Quaker women, also found time to preach at many Quaker meeting houses.

Then, in 1813, she met a French Quaker, Stephen Grellet, who was visiting London. While he was in London, he'd visited a famous prison there, called Newgate. He told Elizabeth what he'd seen: many very sick prisoners, lying on the bare floor or ☞

on some old straw, because there were no beds. Most had only very scanty clothing, even though it was very cold. There were several young children living there, almost naked. They'd been born in prison and spent all their lives in prison, just because their mothers were prisoners. They had done nothing wrong themselves.

Elizabeth said four words. 'Something must be done.' And she got started at once. She gathered together a number of women Quakers and organized a huge sewing party, making clothes for the prisoners. Then, with just one friend, she went to the prison and asked the governor to grant her permission to visit the women prisoners.

He did not think it would be a good idea at all. 'The convicts, ma'am, are very rough. Why, I do not like visiting them myself.'

Elizabeth was having none of that. She insisted on being let in. The governor reluctantly agreed – but had one suggestion. 'Ma'am, pray at least leave your watch outside, for safe keeping – the pickpockets would you know...'

'This watch goes with me everywhere,' she replied. It was one that Joseph had given her before they married.

Elizabeth and her friend were admitted to the prison. Later, she wrote in her diary about what she had seen. 'There were 300 women in two rooms. Some had been sentenced to death. Others were waiting for trial. More than anything, I was moved to see two prisoners tearing the clothes from a baby that had just died to clothe one still alive.'

She also found that the prisoners had to pay for the straw they slept on. So, next day, she returned with clean straw for the sick and more clothes for the prison children. Over the months, her work continued. She decided to form a school in Newgate for the children of the prisoners, as well as for the younger criminals. But she had trouble persuading the governor that this would work.

'It's an admirable plan. It does you credit, Mistress Fry,' he explained. 'But you do not understand the problem. Even the children are vicious. And anyway there is no suitable room.'

Elizabeth wasn't put off so easily. 'Is it only lack of space that prevents the experiment?'

She found a room in the prison that wasn't being used for anything else – so the experiment went ahead. And she also arranged for the women prisoners to do some work in the prison. This was mainly sewing: making patchwork out of scraps of old material – but at least it was something that could be sold outside the prison and earn the women enough to buy clothes and food and soap for themselves and their children.

The Governor was forced to admit the success of Elizabeth Fry's work. 'The benevolent work of Mistress Fry and her friends in the female department of the prison has indeed, by the establishment of a school, by providing work and encouraging industrious habits, produced the most gratifying change.'

Elizabeth Fry became a famous person, known throughout the country. And everywhere she went she preached; for example, in Bridewell Prison in Glasgow. A woman who was present there wrote an account of the visit.

'Mistress Fry took off her bonnet and sat on a low seat facing 100 women prisoners. She took the Bible and read from it. She often paused and looked at the women with tenderness and quickly won their confidence. The reading was followed by a ☛

solemn pause, and then, resting her Bible on the ground, there was Mistress Fry kneeling before the women. Her prayer was beyond words.'

Elizabeth Fry took clothing and other comforts to prisoners all round the country. She persuaded them to follow new rules of behaviour, and in return the authorities promised to improve the conditions of the prison. But her work was not approved of by everyone. In Parliament, they made fun of her ideas; and, in the prisons, inspectors reintroduced severe punishments. Even so she continued to devote her life to prison reform, driven by her concern for people who were suffering more than they deserved.

As she wrote in her diary, 'I desire to do justly, love mercy and walk humbly with my God.' ◆

24

Mary Jones' Bible

Mary Jones was born in 1784 and lived in north-west Wales. The story of her determination to own a copy of the Bible in Welsh led to the foundation of the British and Foreign Bible Society (now known as the Bible Society). The story illustrates the importance of the Bible for Christians and suggests what can be achieved by determination.

Suppose you didn't have to come to school. Suppose you didn't have to learn to read and write. Would you mind? This is the story of a girl who lived when there were very few schools and, more than anything, she wanted to go to one.

There was something else she wanted: a Bible. This is the story of how she managed to get what she wanted – by being really determined.

◆

MARY JONES LIVED with her parents in a tiny Welsh mountain village, where her father made a living by weaving cloth and selling it at a market in a nearby town. They spoke Welsh, not English. Her story begins in the year 1793, when she was nine.

In those days there were few schools in that part of Wales, but there was a little chapel in the nearby village of Abergynolwyn [*say*: aber-guh-nol-win] and every Sunday Mary and her parents went to the service there and, because everyone in the village spoke Welsh, the service was in Welsh.

One Sunday, as the service came to an end, Mary had a sudden thought, which she whispered to her mother. ☛

'Mam, if we had our own Holy Bible back home, it wouldn't be any use.'

Her mother was shocked. 'There's a thing to say, now!'

But Mary was right. A Bible was no use if you couldn't read. And as none of the family could read, they knew what was in the Bible only because it was read to them on Sundays by the minister, Mr Hughes [just as, over 1000 years before, St Aidan had had to tell the people of Northumbria what was in the Bible].

Some time after this, Mary's father came home from market with some rather special news for Mary and her mother. Next week a school was to be opened in Abergynolwyn. Mary was very excited by the idea. 'Mam, Dad, can I go to school? Say I can go to school to learn to read!'

Mary was indeed allowed to go to the little school when it opened – and because she worked hard, after several weeks, she could read quite well. She could even read the Bible, in her own language, Welsh.

Then, one day, she had another idea. 'Why shouldn't I buy my very own Bible? But who ever heard of it? A poor Welsh girl with her own Bible! I'd never save up enough money. And where would I get one from?'

Because apart from the one in the chapel and the one that the schoolteacher had, there wasn't a Welsh Bible in all Abergynolwyn. Even so, Mary Jones started to save. She sold eggs from two hens she had been given, she sold honey from a beehive she owned. She knitted socks and got her father to sell them at market; she grew a few vegetables and sold those too. But it took a long time to fill the money box her father had made for her to keep her savings in. In fact it took six years.

Mary was now fifteen. But one evening, after they had all had supper, Mary opened her money box and counted the coins. She was sure she must have enough.

'That's fine,' said her mother, 'but where are you going to be getting a Bible from? Even if you have got the money?'

'I asked Mr Hughes the preacher,' answered Mary. 'He said there were none for sale in Abergynolwyn, nor in Towyn nor even in Dolgellau [*say*: **dol-geth-lau** (*rhyming with* cow)] —'

'So where are you going to be finding one then?' interrupted her father.

'From Bala.'

But Bala was more than 20 miles away, over the mountains. Mary had been told that in Bala was a gentleman, a Mr Charles, who had got a parcel of Welsh Bibles from London. In the end, she persuaded her parents to let her walk to Bala, even though it might take her two days. Her mother made her a parcel of bread and cheese to eat on the journey.

And so, early one morning, Mary Jones set out to walk to Bala. Sometimes she lost her way. Often she thought she'd never get there. She stopped several times to drink from one of the mountain streams and, whenever she saw anyone, which was only rarely, she stopped to ask the way. It was late evening when she arrived in Bala and found her way to the house of a friend of Mr Hughes the preacher.

Next morning, very early, before there was any chance of Mr Charles having gone out preaching, Mary Jones went to call at his house and told him her story. He was very impressed that she had been prepared to save up for six years, just so she could buy a Bible. ☛

But she was to be disappointed. All the Bibles had been sold. Mr Charles explained why.

'There are schools in many places now, and many boys and girls are learning to read, their parents as well. And they all want Bibles, in their own language. And in London, where they print the Bibles, they print only a very few in Welsh.'

But Mary was not, in the end, to be disappointed.

'After such a walk, Mary Jones, I cannot let you go home without a Bible. I have one left. It was promised for a friend, but he speaks and reads a little English as well as Welsh. So your need is the greater. Take this Bible then, and keep it safely.'

And so Mary Jones got her Welsh Bible. Her journey back home seemed much shorter than the walk to Bala, so excited was she at having her own Bible to show to her parents, and to read to them. As for Mr Charles, he was so impressed by Mary's story and by the number of other people who wanted Welsh Bibles that he travelled to London; and, partly as a result of what he had to say, in 1804, the Bible Society was formed. This society was to provide copies of the Bible in many different languages for people all around the world. ◆

25

Lord Shaftesbury

Anthony Ashley Cooper, seventh Earl of Shaftesbury (1801–85), is remembered for his work in reforming working conditions in factories and coal mines. Among the improvements he secured were the appointment of inspectors to ensure that children under the age of nine were not employed in mills and establishing that women and children should not work in mines. Another of his achievements was to end the use of small boys as climbing chimney sweeps. (As a young man, he had the title Lord Ashley.)

In the year 1815, Anthony Ashley Cooper was only fourteen years old and still a schoolboy. He was also extremely rich. In fact, he was so rich he need never have done a day's work. He could have spent his whole life just enjoying himself. And at fourteen, he was already a lord: Lord Ashley. One day that schoolboy was to see an event which was to change his life and change the lives of thousands of other people. It was a funeral.

◆

YOUNG LORD ASHLEY was at school: a boarding school called Harrow. One afternoon when there were no lessons, he went for a walk – and it was then he saw the funeral. A pauper's funeral. Just three men carrying a coffin, no family, no other people. And the men were staggering about: they were obviously drunk. Young Lord Ashley was angry.

'I say, my good men!' he shouted. 'Show some respect. That's someone's coffin you're carrying.'

'Thish is George,' answered one of the men.

'Thish *was* George,' said another, trying to stand upright. ☛

'But this is no way to conduct a funeral,' said the schoolboy, primly. 'Why can't he have a proper funeral?'

'George died without any money. He's a pauper. So 'e'll be buried in paupers' corner.'

The third man then spoke for the first time. 'It's not a grave, young governor. Just a shallow 'ole, for people with no money. They're not buried proper. Only the rich can afford to be buried. People like yourself. We just tips 'im in the ground.'

Lord Ashley could not forget the sight of that man's funeral. As time went by, he made a resolution. 'When I'm grown up, I shall use my time to help the poor.' So he became a Member of Parliament, and set about finding out about the conditions in which the poor had to earn their living.

In those days, around about the year 1830, even very young children had to work in factories and in weaving and spinning mills. They were made to crawl into the moving machines and to oil and grease them; they were beaten if they stopped work for even a few moments; they became weak and deformed and suffered from terrible diseases. Some were forced to work from six in the morning until half past eight at night, or even later. Their parents did not object: they needed the money.

Lord Ashley knew that all this must be changed. He made a speech about it in Parliament.

'... And so I say, we must, I repeat, we must improve the lives of our workers, especially those of our women and children. This is a Christian country, and every citizen is equal in the sight of Almighty God. They must be treated fairly! They must have time to rest, an hour of leisure once a day. We must put an end to this barbaric treatment of our children.'

Other speakers disagreed. One MP stood up and said, 'My

Lord Ashley argues convincingly but he is wrong. Such changes cannot be. If the workers do not labour such hours, factory profits will fall, owners will be forced to close mills and factories and the workers will lose their jobs. Indeed, the workers themselves welcome this opportunity to earn a wage.'

Lord Ashley tried and tried again. It took many debates like that before any improvement was agreed upon – but, at last, in 1833, an Act of Parliament was passed. The wording was as follows: 'It is hereby enacted that no child of under nine years may be employed at all, and those aged from nine years to thirteen years may not work for more than 48 hours in any one week.'

Gradually more laws were passed. In the end, children were stopped from working down mines, from working up chimneys as chimney sweeps, and in factories. And many of these improvements were the result of Lord Ashley's untiring efforts to work to help the poor.

He started schools, he persuaded the government to build houses for working people and he worked for improvements in hospitals. Then, when he was 50, his father died. His father had been the Earl of Shaftesbury, and so Lord Ashley now became the new Earl of Shaftesbury (or Lord Shaftesbury) – which is the name we remember him by.

When *he* died, a statue was put up in the middle of Piccadilly Circus in London. We call it Eros, but the man who made it called it the Angel of Christian Charity, in honour of the Earl of Shaftesbury. A rich man but not a selfish man; a man who didn't need to do anything but who spent his life working to help others. ◆

26

The underground railroad

Slavery may be defined as 'the enforced servitude of one person to another'. A slave has no rights and is the 'property' of another through birth, purchase or capture. The first black slaves were landed in North America in 1619. As many as 70,000 slaves may have been taken to the Americas in the one year of 1790 alone. They were seen as a vital work-force in the cotton and other plantations.

By 1804, 'abolitionists' in the northern United States had achieved the end of slavery in those states – but it remained lawful in the South. The 'Underground Railroad' was an escape route from the South run by a network of abolitionists. Harriet Tubman's flight to the North took place in 1849. As she became famous, huge rewards were offered for her capture – but she was never caught.

Imagine a railway with no tracks. Just a network of secret paths though woods and fields. Its 'trains' were groups of people walking on foot. If they were seen and caught, they'd be put to death. And instead of stations this railway (or 'railroad', because it was in America) had 'safe houses' and churches – where the 'trains' of people could hide and rest. Because it was secret and hidden, it was called the Underground Railroad. And its heroine was Harriet Tubman.

◆

THIS WAS A time when white people in the southern part of the United States of America owned slaves, black people who had been kidnapped in Africa and brought to America to work for the landowners there. Slaves were treated worse than animals. They were bought and sold at auctions as though they were just 'things'. They were treated harshly and often whipped or caned for the slightest fault. Many slaves dreamed of escaping to the northern part of the country where slavery was against the law.

One such slave was Harriet Tubman. She had to scrub and sweep, plough, chop wood, carry logs – all with very little sleep. She was often beaten and once she was hit on the head with a heavy iron weight for daring to speak up to the man in charge of the slaves.

At last, she could bear it no longer. One summer's night in 1849, she decided to run away. Secretly, she slipped away from her owner's house in Maryland and, with only the Pole Star to guide her, she walked northwards. Although she could not read, she believed in the Bible and she had faith that God would guide her.

Nevertheless, it was a dangerous journey. Armed men on horseback were always on the lookout for escaping slaves. They used bloodhounds to sniff out the tracks of any slave and there were posters offering rewards to anyone who recaptured a 'runaway'.

It was only safe to travel at night. Harriet knew that few people would want to help her: they could be fined 1000 dollars for helping a runaway slave. But at last she reached safety in the state of Pennsylvania in the North. She was free! She got a job as a cook. With pay! Something she'd never had before.

But Harriet Tubman couldn't enjoy her freedom. She was always thinking of her friends who were still slaves, back down south. She wanted to help them to freedom. So she gave up her job and went back to Maryland. Then she guided a whole group of slaves back north, using the safe hiding places she had found on her own journey. She also began to find friendly farmers who would let the escaping slaves hide in a shed or barn during daylight. Even so, it remained very dangerous, ☛

travelling in the dark through swamps and forests. If a baby or young child started to cry and wouldn't stop, it had to be drugged into silence so that no-one would hear.

In the years which followed, Harriet made eighteen more raids and freed over 300 slaves, including her own mother and father. The network of safe tracks and homes and churches of those prepared to help escaping slaves became known as 'the Underground Railroad'. Other 'conductors' began to help and, in the next ten years, many thousands made the difficult journey to freedom, thanks to the 'railroad' and to people like Harriet. In all her journeys, she never lost a single 'passenger'.

She was once asked why she did it all. 'I go only where God sends me,' she said. [She became known as the Moses of her people – because just as Moses had once guided the Israelites out of slavery in Egypt, so she guided her people north out of slavery in the South.] ◆

27

Set free in Freetown

The Yoruba are the majority ethnic group in southwest Nigeria. Samuel Adjai Crowther (a member of that group) was born about 1812, captured when only a child, and was apparently destined for slavery in America. Instead, he was 'set free in Freetown', in Sierra Leone. There he received some education and was then sent to school in London. He returned to Sierra Leone, and later became a priest. He returned to his homeland to teach his own people about Christianity and, in 1864, became the first black bishop. He was also a Doctor of Divinity (Oxford).

It has been estimated that the British slave trade shipped two million slaves from Africa to the West Indies between 1680 and 1786. The British Parliament passed the Abolition of the Slave Trade Act in 1807 which banned the taking of slaves. 'Slavery' (the holding of slaves) was abolished throughout British territory in 1833.

On 29 June 1864 in Canterbury Cathedral, a man called Samuel Adjai Crowther became the first black African to be made a bishop. It was thanks to him that many people in Nigeria first heard about Jesus. It is a story that almost never happened.

◆

ADJAI GREW UP in the Land of the Yoruba River in what is now Nigeria in West Africa. He lived a life like any other boy until he was about ten. Then came the terrible day he was kidnapped.

A group of white men came to his village. Quickly and roughly, they seized Adjai. He was marched to the river and thrown in a boat with some other boys and young men. They were taken down the river towards the sea where a much larger ship was waiting. Soon they were prisoners in the dark depths ☛

of that ship's hold. Adjai did not know what would happen. If he had known, he might have been even more frightened. These men were 'slavers'. They captured strong young Africans, took them by ship across the Atlantic Ocean and sold them as slaves in America. There were laws against it – but that didn't stop them. Something else did, though.

Ships of the British Navy now patrolled the west coast of Africa, trying to catch the slave ships as they left the African coast. Adjai was lucky. The ship he was on *was* stopped and all the Africans on it were taken to a port called Freetown where they were all set free. Freetown is on the coast of a country called Sierra Leone.

It all seemed very strange to the village boy who could neither read nor write. What terrified him most was a butcher's shop with meat hanging up in its window. Adjai was certain that was how he was going to end up. But he was taken care of by a schoolmaster. His wife taught Adjai to read and write and it was here that he first heard about Jesus. Later, the schoolmaster and his wife took Adjai to London where he trained to become a teacher himself – and where he became a Christian.

When he had finished his training, he went back to Sierra Leone and became a village school teacher. But he still had another ambition.

'God has been good to me,' he said, 'so now I must work for him.' He decided to become a priest – which in those days meant going back to study in London. While he was there, he started translating the Bible into the Yoruba language, so that his own people could read it for themselves. And one day, while he was doing that, something quite extraordinary happened.

Adjai was working quietly at his translation in a London

library. Something made him stop as another man, a white man in naval uniform came in, to look something up in a book. Adjai stared at him. This was obviously a very important man: it was an admiral's uniform he was wearing.

Admiral Sir Henry Leeke (that was the man's name) never forgot what happened then.

'I'd just crept in there very quietly, don't you know – so's not to disturb anybody. Then, next thing I know, there's this fellow hugging me, shouting and thanking God!'

Because Adjai had recognised who the admiral was. Years before, Henry Leeke had been the captain of the British ship that had rescued Adjai from a life of slavery. It was a very happy meeting.

Later, when he'd become a priest, Adjai went back to his own country, the Land of the Yoruba, and travelled by boat along its rivers. He stopped at each village to tell the people about Jesus. They respected him because he was from that country himself and many people believed what he taught and became Christians.

He came back to England once again, though. In the year 1864, in Canterbury Cathedral, he was made a bishop: the first black African bishop. And among those who came to be with Bishop Adjai in the cathedral on that special day were the schoolmaster and his wife from Freetown who had first taught Adjai – and also Admiral Sir Henry Leeke.

Adjai was very pleased and grateful for all the help he'd received during his life. To show his thanks, he worked hard in the Land of the Yoruba and, by the time he died in 1891, many of the villages had their own schools. Adjai had been determined that, in future, it should not be just a matter of luck whether Yoruba children should have the chance to learn to read and write – and to hear about things that matter. ◆

28

George and the chocolate factory

This story outlines the work of the Quaker philanthropist, George Cadbury (1839–1922). Besides expanding his father's chocolate business, he planned and developed the first 'model' village. At a time when many employers exploited their workers, Cadbury showed care and concern for their welfare, in and out of the work place.

Dairy Milk Chocolate. Milk Tray. Chocolate Cream Eggs. Cadbury's Flake. Yes, today's story is all about chocolate and the man who ran the firm that makes those brands: George Cadbury. But we begin with his father and an advertisement for his firm.

◆

'JOHN CADBURY'S OF 93 Bull Street, Birmingham. Tea and coffee dealer. Also cocoa; prepared by myself; a most nutritious breakfast beverage; no chemicals used; absolutely pure; Cadbury of Bull Street.'

If you'd lived in Birmingham nearly 200 years ago, then that was an advert you might have seen in the local paper, put there by John Cadbury whose business was making and selling cocoa. As it said in the advert, cocoa was a new breakfast drink or 'beverage'. John was pleased it became very popular not just because it made him money but because he thought alcoholic drinks were wrong. In those days, even at breakfast time, most people (children included) drank beer! (One reason for this was the fact that the water wasn't clean enough to drink safely.)

Shortly after this, John Cadbury retired. His two sons, Richard (who was 25) and George (who was 21) took over the factory where they made the cocoa, and also chocolate.

Richard and George employed more workers. And they cared about their workers. Until then, all factory workers had to work six full days a week. Cadbury's was the first firm in Birmingham to introduce a Saturday half holiday; and, when it was frosty, they gave the men time off to go skating! As George Cadbury said, 'Sport is good for a man. As is fresh air.' So he also arranged outings for his workers to the countryside.

It was after one of these trips that he got a new idea. Instead of having factories in the centres of cities, amongst all the slums and smoke and grime, why shouldn't there be a factory in a garden? A garden factory!

He knew an ideal place as well. Four miles south of the city, beside the Worcester Canal which meant that barges could bring the cocoa direct from where it was unloaded from the ships in Bristol docks; and it was also near the new railway line from Birmingham so the workers could travel easily to the factory. What's more, George arranged special cheap fares for them: what were called 'workmen's returns'.

George and Richard built a canteen where their workers could have a midday meal – something no factory owners had thought of providing until then. All they needed now was a name for this new 'ideal' factory. George had a discussion with his brother Richard.

'We could call it after that little stream – you know, the one near by. Bourn Brook.'

'So we'd call it Bourn Factory,' suggested Richard. 'No,' he said, changing his mind. 'It's more like a little town. Bourn Town.'

'I think a French name would be more sensible,' replied George.

'What makes you say that?'

'People think French chocolate is best. You know, smarter.'

'So we'll use the French word for town. *Ville*.

'That's it. Bournville!'

The factory in the garden was a great success. When the Cadburys moved there in 1879, they had 230 workers. Twenty years later, there were nearly 3000 workers – all making drinking cocoa and chocolate. The Cadburys were getting very rich; but there was one sadness: Richard died of a disease called diphtheria while he was on holiday abroad. George carried on running his factory. But something still worried him: the houses his workers had to live in, in the poorer parts of Birmingham.

'They're so clustered in upon each other, long terraces of them, built back to back and facing onto a tiny narrow street. Down its middle, a gutter forces its way... Women throw household slops of every description into that gutter... And their houses are tiny, and very dark inside because the window panes are broken and blocked up with rags. And the smell is dreadful! Do you know, in two small rooms, there live nine people. In the rooms upstairs, two other families... It's terrible.'

Not every factory owner worried like this about where and how his workers lived. But George Cadbury did. He was also worried that more and more of these slums were being built, spreading outwards from the centre of Birmingham. So, with his own money, he bought a lot of land near his factory and began to plan Bournville Village.

Each house was to have a garden, three times the area of the house. Each house was to be in the shape of a country cottage;

some being of brick, some of black and white timber construction. He took great care to preserve all the trees on the site and others were planted along the new roads.

George arranged for much more to be done at Bournville. He had schools built; museums, a hospital and parks. He himself taught in a school for grown-ups who'd had to leave school when they were only eleven or twelve. And he arranged holidays for poor children from Birmingham, even if they were nothing to do with his firm. But *why*? Why did he do this? Did he perhaps feel guilty or embarrassed because he had become so rich?

He did it because he was a Quaker. Quakers are Christians who are members of the 'Society of Friends'. For them, religion isn't just something you do one day a week, at church. Religion is what you do all the time. This is a question that Quakers are meant to ask themselves: 'Do you, as followers of Jesus Christ ... seek to promote the welfare of those in any kind of need?'

George Cadbury could answer 'Yes'. For him, his Christian faith meant building proper houses for his workers, giving them a good place to live; *and* helping all the people in the area in which he lived. As well as making chocolate. ◆

29

Honest Jesse

Jesse Boot (1850–1931) was born in Nottingham, the son of John Boot, a herbalist and Methodist lay preacher. When Jesse was ten, his father died and Jesse left school to help his mother gather herbs to sell in their small shop which provided natural remedies for the poor in the working-class district in which they lived. But the working classes were being seduced by the new so-called 'patent' medicines, many of which were of little value. The quick-witted (and honest) Jesse Boot realized he could help the people around him and build up a thriving retail business (which later expanded into drug manufacturing as well). He used his wealth to create parks and hospital wards and to benefit University College, Nottingham.

One shop most of us need at some time or other is a chemist. And in almost every big shopping centre, you'll see one particular chemist's shop: Boots the Chemists. It was started by a man called Jesse Boot and among the first medicines he sold were, would you believe, wild flowers and nettles.

◆

BACK IN THE year 1860, in a country lane not far from Nottingham, you might have seen a ten-year-old boy and his mother gathering flowers and herbs and, yes, nettles. They were young Jesse Boot and his mother. They went out gathering these plants two days a week. The other days of the week, they ran a little shop; just the two of them, because Jesse's father had died earlier that year.

In those days, before modern medicines had been invented, people made medicines from different plants, using special recipes to make these 'herbal medicines' – which is what Jesse's mother did and what Jesse was learning to do. And then they sold them in their shop.

But as Jesse grew up, what were called 'patent medicines' began to be sold: bottles of sweet syrup and boxes of pills. 'For the head and stomach' said one box. 'For the blood and stomach' said another. But whatever their aim, all these new pills contained the *same* ingredients. Soap and a mild laxative. That was all. But they did differ in colour. Some were red, some green, others pink. And people bought them, thinking they would cure their illnesses.

There were *some* good new medicines on the market though, and Jesse Boot decided to sell these – but at much less than they were being sold in other shops. He was determined to be fair to his customers. Even so, the shop's weekly takings went up from £20 to £100. But as he once said: 'There's nothing remarkable about my methods. It's simply common sense. I found that everywhere medicines were being sold at ridiculously high prices. And sold without any regard at all for neatness – or attractiveness. My idea was simply to buy tons of the stuff so I could buy more cheaply *and* sell more cheaply. With some of these medicines, you know, I found I could knock two pence off the price other shops charged, and still make a nice little profit!'

And so Jesse Boot's business grew and grew. He opened more and more shops and took on extra staff to help. He began to sell other things – like soap. The ordinary price in those days was four pence. Mr Boot offered it at four pence halfpenny for two pieces. He packed them up in a nicely shaped parcel, tied up neatly with string *and* labelled. Then there were the tins of salmon. He once bought a huge quantity. The price at that time was eight pence a tin. Mr Boot's price was four pence halfpenny. As the news went round, people rushed to buy ☛

asking, 'A tin of salmon, please, and will you open it?' Because as Jesse Boot explained later, 'You see, tin openers weren't to be found in every house in them times. Oh no, people weren't well off then.'

So 'Boots the Chemists' as the shops were becoming known, sold different things at low prices, which helped the poor – and it all made Jesse Boot very rich. But he also worked very hard. He worked sixteen hours every day except Sundays when he went to church and took some exercise in the country. He once looked back on his life: 'They all said I might be honest, but I wouldn't make money. Well, I've made money.' So how did he use his money?

Jesse Boot gave away over two million pounds. Half of it, he gave so that what is now Nottingham University could be built. He paid for new chapels in the poorer parts of Nottingham. He gave a quarter of a million pounds to pay for a new park; £50,000 for Nottingham General Hospital.

So, what do you think of Jesse Boot? Not everyone liked this very rich business man who seemed to think only about work and his factory and shops. But others knew he was a religious man, a good man and an honest one. ◆

30

Quite ordinary

Thérèse Martin was born in northern France in 1873, the daughter of a watchmaker (five of whose daughters became nuns). In 1888 she entered the Carmelite convent of Lisieux in Normandy where two of her sisters were already nuns. Her life there was uneventful, 'ordinary' – and short. She died nine years later of tuberculosis in 1897. After her death, her 'little way', a book (first called The Story of a Soul *and later* The Autobiography of a Saint*) had a sensational success and she was made a saint in 1925. Her life story has been a comfort and an inspiration to millions of (especially Catholic) Christians in that it shows everyone can serve God and their neighbours by doing everyday things in a spirit of love and kindness.*

So who was Thérèse Martin? Well, for a start, she didn't live very long. She died when she was only 24.

So what did she do?

Not a lot. In fact, not very much at all.

So was she special?

No: quite ordinary, really, and that's why she's become famous, very famous. And why she was made a saint. If you like, she was 'picked out' as a very holy person, a good person. But she wasn't always like that.

◆

THERESE MARTIN WAS born over 100 years ago. She lived in a town in northern France called Lisieux. Her mother had died when she was quite young and she lived with her father and her four older sisters.

Marie, the oldest of the sisters, became a sort of mother to the family. Except to little Thérèse. *She* turned instead to her next-oldest sister, Pauline.

☛

'You're *my* mother now,' she said.

And Pauline did take special care of Thérèse. In fact, perhaps because Thérèse was the youngest and because she was often ill, they all rather spoilt her.

Once, Léonie (who was the middle sister) came along with a basket of dolls and sewing things she no longer wanted. 'Here,' she said to the two youngest sisters. 'Choose which of these you'd like.' When it was Thérèse's turn to choose, she thought for a moment and then said, 'I choose the lot.'

She got them all, as well.

And if things didn't go how she wanted, Thérèse would burst into tears. There were several times when she deliberately 'cried', just so she would get her own way. But when she was eight, something happened that really did upset her. Her favourite older sister Pauline decided to become a nun and go and live in a convent in Lisieux. But this was a special kind of convent, where the nuns didn't just live when they weren't out teaching or nursing or whatever. Once they went in, they stayed in. All the time.

This group of nuns (called Carmelite nuns) believe that, by staying in 'Carmel' (as they call it), they can do more for people by praying for them than by doing anything else. And as they are allowed very few visitors, Thérèse was incredibly miserable about 'losing' Pauline.

The years went by. Thérèse was slowly getting used to life without Pauline. Then, when she was thirteen, her oldest sister Marie said that she too was 'going into Carmel'. There were more tears. Lots more tears.

But that Christmas, things changed. When they had been little, all the Martin sisters were given their Christmas presents after they got back from church. They would come home and each of them would find their presents tucked inside a pair of their own boots, in a special corner of the house. It was a family custom. By now all the sisters had grown out of it – except Thérèse. But this year, just as she got into the house, she overheard her father saying, 'Oh, this is far too babyish for a girl like Thérèse. I hope it's the last time we have to do it.'

He didn't mean her to hear him – but she did. Again she started to cry and sulk. Then something stopped her. At that moment, she knew she must stop thinking just of herself, of what *she* wanted. It was time to grow up.

And soon she made another decision: like her elder sisters, she too would enter Carmel.

At first there were problems. People said Thérèse was too young to enter Carmel. But that autumn, her father took her on a visit to Rome. She was allowed to see the Pope, to be blessed by him. And when she was kneeling before him, even though she wasn't supposed to say anything, Thérèse spoke up. 'Holy father,' she said, 'allow me to enter Carmel.'

The Pope seemed unsure what to say to this young girl. At last he said, 'If it be God's will.'

So in the year 1888, at the age of fifteen, Thérèse entered Carmel. The doors closed behind her, shutting out her father and the rest of the family. 'I'm here for good, now; here for good!' she thought. And she was happy.

But even though she was near her older sisters again, not everything was easy. Whenever Thérèse took her turn at doing the housework around the convent or weeding its garden, one of the older Carmelite nuns would always criticise her. 'This child does absolutely nothing! Nothing at all.' ☞

Gradually, Thérèse learned not to answer back. One of the first times she managed this was when someone else had left a little jar by a window and it had got broken. One of the other nuns supposed it had been Thérèse's fault. 'You mustn't be so untidy. You must be much more careful!'

Thérèse didn't answer back: she just said she was sorry.

And so, in little ways like this, Thérèse learned to be patient and unselfish. In summer, when it was hot, she did her washing in the laundry room where it was very stuffy, so others could use a cooler room; and in winter, she'd use the cold tap so others could use the hot water. And she'd always eat whatever food was put in front of her without complaining, no matter how awful or how old it was.

After five years, Thérèse's sister, Pauline, became prioress, or leader, of the nuns and one evening she and Marie were talking with Thérèse about when they were children. Pauline told Thérèse to write down her memories. At first, Thérèse didn't want to, but obediently she agreed to do so. She had very little spare time, so it took her over a year, and when she'd finished it, she gave it to Pauline.

Pauline showed it to Marie. Both sisters were very impressed but they felt that Thérèse should write more about her 'little way'; that is, her way of pleasing God by doing little things for other people and by putting up with things without complaining.

But by now, Thérèse was ill. Seriously ill this time, with an illness called tuberculosis, for which there was no cure in those days.

Marie encouraged Thérèse to finish her story. Even though Thérèse was in great pain, she did so – without complaining.

Indeed, she managed to keep so calm and to smile so much that few of the others knew how much she was suffering. She finished her writing in July, 1897, two months before she died.

After her death, her book was published. Since then, it's sold millions of copies, all round the world.

And why?

Well, because Thérèse of Lisieux showed that ordinary people can become special, can become saints, by following her 'little way'. You don't have to be out-of-the-ordinary to help others and to please God. ◆

31

The hiding place

Corrie ten Boom was born in Haarlem in the Netherlands in 1892. She and her older sister, Betsie, were both Christians. During World War II they helped many Jews to avoid capture by the Nazis. They were themselves arrested for this and sent to Ravensbrück concentration camp in East Germany.

It's not easy to help someone who's in danger. You might get into danger yourself. This story is about two very brave sisters who were ready to take that risk.

It happened in 1940, when there was war all over Europe. Nazi soldiers from Germany had invaded Holland, and treated the people of that country very cruelly. They were especially cruel to any Jewish people they found.

The two sisters were Corrie and Betsie ten Boom. They were both about 50, but Corrie was two years younger than Betsie. They were watchmakers and lived in a house over their shop in the town of Haarlem. As they were Christians, not Jews, they might have been safe from the Nazis...

◆

IT ALL BEGAN with a man who had two large bulldogs. Because Corrie and Betsie had never seen him without them, they privately nicknamed him 'the Bulldog'. But one day, they did see him without his dogs. Corrie went up to him in the street.

'Please, where are your dogs? Are they all right?' The man looked very tearful.

'Are they all right?' he repeated. 'They are ... they are dead. I put the "medicine" in their bowl myself. Then I stroked them to sleep. They died very peacefully.'

'But why did you kill them? Was it because of the rationing?' asked Corrie. 'We could have got food for them.'

'Ladies, I am a Jew. You know what the Nazis are like. Soon they will take me away to prison. Or worse. Then who would look after my dogs?'

Corrie and Betsie became good friends with the man. He visited their house and other Jewish people came too. The two sisters heard how the Nazis attacked Jews for no reason and how shopkeepers were made to put up signs saying 'Jews will not be served here'. They realized that the Nazi soldiers would soon send all their new Jewish friends away to prison camps, perhaps to be put to death – for no reason except that they were Jewish. So they got a good friend to make a secret room for them, on the top floor of their house. It was made by building a false wall which divided Corrie's bedroom in half. Their friend painted the wall and then made it dirty, so it looked as if it had always been there. There was a secret panel by which you could get into this hiding place – which may have been rather small but which was at least somewhere where their friends could hide, if the Nazis came to search the house.

And one night, the soldiers did come.

'Get up! Come on, up!' they shouted. Corrie struggled out of bed. 'Tell us, where are you hiding the Jews?'

'There aren't any Jews here,' said Corrie. 'Just me and my sister.'

'Where's your secret room?'

'Lord Jesus, help me now,' whispered Corrie to herself. But she didn't answer.

The soldiers seized her by the elbow and pushed her downstairs into the shop. Another soldier was guarding Betsie. ☛

Corrie saw that her lips were swollen and there was a dark bruise near her eye.

'If you don't tell us where the room is, we'll set a guard round the house until your Jews starve to death. Now, where are they?'

Corrie and Betsie still said nothing. They were both taken away and put in separate prison cells in the Nazi headquarters in Holland, knowing nothing about what had happened to the Jews in their hiding place.

Many weeks after they were put in prison, Corrie was allowed a visitor: her brother Willem who also lived in Haarlem. A soldier stood guard, listening all the time, while they had a short conversation.

'I want you to know, Corrie,' said Willem, 'that all your watches are safe.'

'What do I care about watches? Or the shop?'

'Corrie,' said Willem, glancing at the guard, 'I mean the "watches" that were in the cupboard upstairs…'

'Oh!' said Corrie, realizing that he was really talking about her Jewish friends. 'Oh dear Jesus, thank you. Thank you, Jesus.'

Months later, Corrie was taken with many other prisoners to a railway yard. They were all herded towards a train. As they were pushed forwards, Corrie suddenly saw Betsie! She wriggled and pushed through the crowd until they were able to grasp each other by the hand. They were together again!

The train was just a lot of vans and cattle trucks. It took them to a place called Ravensbrück, a women's prison camp in Germany where many prisoners were put to death.

The days passed. The two sisters suffered from the cold winter, from beatings and from hunger. One thing gave them hope. Corrie had been able to smuggle a small Bible with her into prison. At night, huddled round a tiny fire, Corrie and Betsie read from it to the other prisoners.

Later, they were moved into another building.

'Betsie!' screamed Corrie. 'Look! Fleas! It's swarming with them. How can we live in here?'

'The answer's in the Bible,' said Betsie. 'It says, "Give thanks always." Give thanks that we're still together. Give thanks that we've still got a copy of the Bible. And that it's crowded in here.'

'Why should we be grateful it's crowded?'

'Because,' said Betsie, 'more prisoners will hear the Bible stories. And we should give thanks for the fleas.'

'Give thanks for the fleas? I can't do that!'

'As long as there are fleas, the Nazis'll keep away and we can say prayers without being disturbed.'

Corrie and Betsie were able to encourage and help many of the other prisoners in Ravensbrück. Eventually, Betsie died there but, towards the end of the war, Corrie was released. She managed to get back to Holland. She went on telling people about how Jesus gave her strength and hope, even in Ravensbrück. She need never have been sent there – but she'd been prepared to suffer all that hardship for doing what she knew was good and right. ◆

32

Crooked Nose

At the end of World War II, hundreds of homeless young men and boys roamed the streets of Naples, mainly in gangs. They spent their lives begging, stealing, fighting and sleeping rough. Always on the move, they became known as the scugnizzi, *the 'spinning tops'. Father Mario Borrelli (who had only recently been made a priest) set out to win their confidence and trust, and to provide a home for them in a disused church.*

Imagine a city street. It's late at night. Dark. Dangerous. A young stranger sits on the edge of the pavement. He's alone. It's quiet. Then, from the far end of the street, a gang of teenage boys appears. The gang's got a leader. A tough lad, his nickname's Fatty – but this story is about the stranger and what he was doing there.

◆

SLOWLY, QUIETLY, THE gang walked up to the stranger.

'I'm the leader round here,' said Fatty to the young stranger. 'And who are you?'

There was a pause. Then the newcomer stood up and spat in Fatty's face and, quickly putting his hands in his pockets, stood there defiantly.

Fatty grinned and pulled a razor-sharp knife from his pocket. 'I'd have cut you up if you hadn't been quicker to get your hand to your knife.' He pointed to the stranger's pocket. 'You'd better join my gang,' he added.

They were all known by nicknames so they called the stranger Crooked Nose. He never let on that, on that first night, his pocket had been empty: he had no knife. Nor did this fair-haired youth (or was he really a young man?) say that he was not really a homeless thug – but a priest.

So what was he doing, in disguise, in the streets of the Italian city of Naples?

At the end of World War II, there were hundreds of homeless young men and boys in Naples. Many had lost their parents in the war. Others had run away from home. Some had been thrown out of their homes by their parents because their tiny houses were getting too crowded with other, younger children. They spent their lives begging, stealing and sleeping in the streets.

Father Mario Borrelli (that was Crooked Nose's real name) had only just become a priest. And he'd decided he must help the homeless boys of Naples who suffered so much from cold, hunger and illness, and especially the younger ones who were regularly beaten up by the older ones. His plan was to make a home for them. But he knew they were afraid of priests, just as much as they were afraid of the police. So every night he disguised himself in filthy old clothes and roamed the streets with Fatty's gang – so that they would think he was just like them and would begin to trust him. They had no idea that during the day he worked as a priest, saying services in church and teaching. The gang just thought he went off on his own to work as a pickpocket.

Meanwhile some other priests and friends of Father Borrelli were repairing and cleaning a disused church. They built a kitchen in it and collected blankets and old beds. Then, one of these helpers (called Salvatore) visited the gang to try to persuade them to come to the church, not letting on he knew who Crooked Nose really was. ☛

'Winter must be a bad time for you boys,' he said. 'With no-where to sleep.'

'We find somewhere,' said one of the gang.

'Not always,' Crooked Nose pointed out. 'Remember that time the police kept us on the move all night.'

'Generally we find a place,' said another.

'I know a place,' said Salvatore. 'An old church, with a roof. And beds.'

'Priests! We're not going to get mixed up with them,' said Fatty.

'No harm in trying it,' said Crooked Nose.

But nothing more was said that night. Even so, Father Borrelli was glad no-one had said a definite 'no' to the idea.

Another night, soon after this, when the church was ready, Father Borrelli went to join the gang as usual. But this time he went dressed as a priest and not in his filthy street clothes – and at first he wasn't recognized. But when they realized this priest was actually their friend Crooked Nose, they weren't angry at being tricked. They were pleased at all he'd put up with, just because he wanted to help them.

And because they still trusted him, they went with him to the church. Another gang came the next night. It became known as the House of the Urchins. Some of the boys were taught trades. Some even got jobs. Another 'home' was opened – so Crooked Nose's plan was all a great success. Except, of course, that even today there are still many homeless young people in cities all around the world. There's still work to be done by people like Crooked Nose.

And why did they give him that nickname? Well, when he was very much younger, his nose got broken. It got better but it mended a bit out of line – and that was how Father Borrelli became known as Crooked Nose. ◆

33

An unbelievably brave man

Leonard Cheshire was born in 1917 and died in 1992. As a bomber pilot in World War II, he flew over 100 missions and was awarded the VC. In 1945, he was Britain's official observer at the dropping of the atom bomb on Nagasaki. After the war, he devoted himself to social work and found his faith by helping the sick (something he was initially very reluctant to undertake).

This is the story of a very brave man who was a bomber pilot during World War II. Many people think he should now be called a saint – not because of what he did in the war but because of what he did afterwards. It was something which, in a way, for him took just as much courage.

◆

TWELVE BOMBER AIRCRAFT flew steadily through the moonlit sky, their engines droning faithfully. They were British bombers, flying over France, making for a town called Limoges.

All this was 50 years ago, during World War II – when Britain was at war with Germany, and the German army had occupied France. That meant that German soldiers were everywhere in France – forcing many French people to work for them.

And that was what had happened at Limoges. There, the Germans had set up a factory to build aircraft engines to use in planes that would attack Britain. No wonder the British wanted to bomb it before any of these engines could be built.

But the Germans were forcing 300 French women to work through each night in the factory, making the aircraft engines.

So what would happen to the French women when the factory was bombed?

The pilot of the leading aircraft had a plan. He was known to all his friends as 'Chesh'. His proper name was Group Captain Leonard Cheshire.

All the lights were on in the factory at Limoges, and Chesh had no trouble in spotting it. But instead of bombing it straight away, he dived in low – his plane hurtling noisily over its roof. He turned his aircraft, saw all the factory lights go off – and zoomed low over it again. This time, in the moonlight, he saw the women running away as fast as they could, away from the building.

There was every chance the Germans would have time to get to their huge guns and shoot his plane down. Even so, Chesh dived a third and fourth time to give the French time to escape. Only then did the twelve Lancaster aircraft drop their heavy bombs on the factory – and then fly safely back to Britain.

Next morning, a small aircraft flew high over Limoges and reported back that the German factory had been totally destroyed. A few weeks later, a secret message reached England from the French workers thanking the bomber pilots for the warning Chesh had given them.

After Britain had defeated Germany and the war was over, what was Chesh to do?

He had the idea of buying a big house called Le Court at Liss in Hampshire. He made it into a home for people who had been soldiers or sailors or airmen during the war but who now had no family and nowhere to live. All went well at first but, after a year, they owed so much money that they had to sell most of the garden around the house and all the people (except Chesh) had to move away.

At this time, Chesh found he was thinking more and more about God and who he was or what he was. Chesh kept remembering one evening during the war. He had been drinking in a night-club in London where some people near him were talking about God. He joined in their conversation: 'God is just another word for our conscience. It's only a voice that tells us what's right and wrong.' 'Nonsense,' said a woman who was there. 'God is real.'

And that was what Chesh was thinking about now. And he was also worrying about one of the men who used to share Le Court with him who was now very ill and in hospital.

This man was called Arthur Dykes. Chesh went to see him. He was horrified to discover that Arthur was so ill there was no hope of his ever getting better. And because of this, the people at the hospital wanted Arthur to leave. They wanted to use the bed for someone they could cure.

But Arthur had no family. No relatives. Where could he go to die?

Chesh decided he would look after Arthur himself.

He wasn't very keen on the idea. Although he had been very brave during the war, he didn't like the idea of caring for a very ill person and being with them when they died. That seemed more frightening than anything he'd done in the war.

Even so, he brought Arthur back to Le Court and began to look after him; to wash him and feed him – and when Arthur became very weak, Chesh had to lift him in and out of bed and help him to do everything.

Then, one day, the telephone rang. It was someone in London who had heard that Chesh was looking after Arthur and wondered if he could also look after another old person as well.

Next day, an ambulance brought an old lady called 'Granny' Haynes to Le Court. She was 94 and so weak that she, too, needed everything doing for her. She was Leonard Cheshire's second patient.

By now, Arthur knew he was dying but, because he was a very religious person, he was not afraid. He knew he would go to Heaven when he died – and Chesh became very interested in Arthur's sure and certain faith.

Then came the day when Arthur did die. While Chesh was waiting for the doctor to come to sign a form that has to be signed whenever someone dies, he picked up a book that Arthur had been reading. It was all about how another man had become a Roman Catholic Christian (like Arthur). Chesh was very impressed and he talked to the local priest about the Church and what it meant to be a Christian. Shortly afterwards, Chesh became a member of the Catholic Church.

By now, many more old and sick people had been brought to stay at Le Court. Leonard Cheshire needed help in looking after them and so a group of people formed a committee to help run what was becoming known as 'the Cheshire Home'.

Chesh was horrified at this name. He didn't want to become famous for all his good work – but he was famous (because of what he had done in the war) and since people knew about him, they were prepared to give money to help run 'the Cheshire Home'.

Soon, a second home was opened in Cornwall and it was shortly after this that he decided he would devote the rest of his life to helping the old, the seriously ill and the handicapped. He decided this because of what he had read in the Bible and because of what he felt his Church was telling him to do – but he never forced his religious beliefs on those he helped. ☞

More and more new homes were started and there are now 270 Cheshire Homes all around the world.

When Leonard Cheshire himself died, a church service was held in London to give thanks for all he had done to help others. At it, someone said he had been 'an unbelievably brave man'. A brave airman, yes, everyone knew that. But Chesh was also brave because he'd done what he hadn't really fancied doing: looking after people who were old and tired and ill. To do something you don't like doing (but which you know should be done), well, that's real bravery. ◆

34

All are welcome

Mother Teresa was born of Albanian parents in Skopje (in Macedonia, formerly part of Yugoslavia) in 1910. While still at school, she heard of a group of nuns working in India. She joined their Order (at first in Ireland) in 1928, at the age of eighteen. The following year she was sent to work in India. She left their convent after eighteen years to start, first, a school for the poorest children in Calcutta and, later, her Home for the Dying. The nuns who have worked with Mother Teresa are known as the Sisters of Charity.

Agnes was twelve when she decided [like Thérèse of Lisieux] that she wanted to be a nun when she grew up and to live in a convent. And, seven years later, that's what she did. First, in Ireland and then, soon after, in India. But eighteen years later, she left her convent to work in the slums of Calcutta, out there in India.

The new name she had taken when she became a nun was Teresa: we know her as Mother Teresa.

◆

SO HOW WAS it that, after eighteen years, Mother Teresa decided she wanted to leave the convent where she lived with all the other nuns? It had been a good time. The work she'd been given to do (as a nun) was teaching geography in a school called St Mary's High School, in Calcutta in India. And, when she wasn't teaching, she lived in the convent which was surrounded by the most beautiful gardens. She'd even become Principal or Headteacher of the school.

Well, it happened one day in 1946: 10 September, to be exact. She was on a train journey when she seemed to hear Jesus speaking to her. 'I heard the call to give up everything and ☛

follow him into the slums, to serve him among the poorest of the poor.'

She was later to call that day her 'Day of Decision'.

It took some time to get permission to leave the convent but, in 1948, she was allowed to leave. She gave up wearing the dark clothes worn by the other nuns and started wearing a sari, like an Indian woman – except that her sari was white with a blue border and with a cross on her shoulder.

Soon, she got other people to help her and they started a school for the very poorest children in Calcutta.

Some time later, in one of the dirtiest and poorest streets of Calcutta, she came across a woman lying in the street, dying. She was so feeble that her body had been partly eaten away by rats and ants, even though she was still just alive. She'd been lying there for days but no-one had taken any notice. Mother Teresa had no trouble in picking her up and carrying her to a nearby hospital. The people there told Mother Teresa that the woman was too ill and too poor for them to bother about. There was no persuading them to look after her but Mother Teresa didn't give up. She took the old woman to another hospital. It was the same there. 'We haven't any room for someone like that,' they said. In the end, the old woman died.

Calcutta was full of people like that. Mother Teresa knew she must help them. She got permission to use part of a building which had once been a Hindu temple but was not now used by anyone except a few thugs and beggars as a place for gambling and drinking. It was to become Mother Teresa's first 'Home for the Dying'.

Since then, Mother Teresa and her helpers have taken in thousands of dying, homeless people. They now have more than

700 shelters in India alone, like that first one; and there are others in Venezuela, Sri Lanka, Tanzania, in all sorts of countries around the world.

Some people have said that Mother Teresa could have done other things that were of more use. They have said that she or her helpers sometimes try to persuade old and weak people to become Christians when that is not their religion.

Mother Teresa once told how she picked a little feeble old woman out of a dustbin. The woman said her son had put her there to die. 'We took her home to our place and we helped her. After a few hours she died in great peace.'

Even though that woman died, Mother Teresa was pleased to have helped her. 'We have homes for the sick and dying and it is beautiful to see how these people, who have lived such difficult lives, die so peacefully.' Mother Teresa calls dying 'going home' – because she believes that people, when they die, go 'home' to be with God.

Of course, many of the people that she has helped got better. Some went to live in comfortable homes. Others even became strong enough to work again. But what Mother Teresa and her helpers have always wanted is to let homeless, sick and dying people know that there is someone who loves them, someone who *wants* them. They help all who are in need: not just Christians, but Hindus, Muslims and Sikhs. All are welcome.

Many people have admired Mother Teresa. In 1979, she won the Nobel Prize and the Pope gave her a special prize for her work. But she once said it is not 'her' work. She was simply continuing the work of Jesus: helping the hungry, the sick and the homeless. ◆

35

Rama and Sita

Hindus believe in one great power called Brahman – and in reincarnation. The aim of every Hindu is to become so good that he or she will eventually escape the cycle of death and rebirth to become part of Brahman. He or she is helped in this aim by the gods and goddesses of Hinduism. One of these is the god Vishnu who once came to earth as Prince Rama. His story is remembered at Divali, a Hindu festival which occurs in late October or early November.

This is a story from India and it is often told at the [*or*: this] time of the year when Hindus celebrate a festival called Divali. It's a story about Prince Rama who lived long ago in a city called Ayodhya. In fact, he was the king's eldest son.

Now, through no fault of his own, when his father died, jealous people stopped Rama from becoming King of Ayodhya and, what was worse, they made him leave the city and go and live for fourteen years in a huge forest. But he didn't go alone. His beautiful wife Sita chose to go with him, and so too did his brother Lakshmana – and that's where our story begins.

◆

FOR MANY YEARS, Rama and Sita lived in the forest, together with Lakshmana, and there they had many adventures and faced many dangers – but none was more exciting or more dangerous than the one I'm about to tell you.

Because, within that forest, there also lived many demons. Now, the king of the demons was called Ravana. He was no ordinary demon for he had the power to turn himself into any shape he wished – and of course that meant he could play all kinds of mean and wicked tricks.

Ravana knew that Rama and Sita were living in what he called 'his' forest and he had seen that Sita was very beautiful indeed. He wanted her to be his wife and so he began to plot. How could he get her away from Rama and take her somewhere where Rama could never reach her?

At last he thought of a plan. The perfect plan! He waited until Rama went out hunting for food. Then he changed himself into a golden-coloured deer. In this shape, he ran through the forest and got just close enough to Rama for Rama to glimpse him through the undergrowth. Rama began to track the deer. Deeper and deeper into the forest went Ravana, still disguised as the deer, and deeper and deeper into the forest followed Rama. Before long, they were in the very thickest part of the forest. Rama then realised he had been so keen to catch the deer that he'd not marked the way he'd come – and so there he was, lost in the middle of the forest, not knowing quite what to do.

Ravana knew exactly what to do. He gave a great shout of 'Help!' – but in Rama's voice! And he used his magic powers to make the shout travel back through the trees to where Sita and Lakshmana were waiting anxiously.

'Lakshmana, it's Rama. He needs help,' begged Sita. 'Please, Lakshmana!'

For a moment, Lakshmana hesitated. Should he stay and protect Sita – or should he rescue Rama?

'Please!' said Sita again. 'Please go!'

So he did. Which was exactly what Ravana had hoped would happen. As soon as Lakshmana was out of the way, Ravana magicked himself back to where Sita was. He was really looking forward to his next trick!

This time, he changed himself into an old holy beggarman, ☛

making himself look very tired and thirsty. As soon as Sita saw him, she wanted to help. 'Surely,' she said to herself, 'there can be no harm in helping a poor old man such as this?' So she called, 'What do you want, Old Man?'

And in the tired voice of a very old man, Ravana croaked, 'Will you help a holy man? Just a little water, if it please you…'

Just as she was getting the water, he changed himself back into his demon shape, seized her, dragged her to a magic chariot he had hidden nearby and drove off – far, far away to a palace he had on an island called Lanka (which is the place we now call Sri Lanka).

When Rama and Lakshmana eventually returned, of course they couldn't find Sita. Rama called her name. No answer. He called again. Still no answer. By now Rama was heartbroken and very sad that he'd been tempted to go so far away in his hunt for the golden deer. But help *was* at hand.

During their time in the forest, Rama and Sita had made friends with many animals – and a very special friend was a monkey called Hanuman. Now Hanuman was no ordinary monkey but the powerful leader of a whole troupe of monkeys. He called these monkeys together and Rama told them how Sita was missing. Off the monkeys went, swinging through the trees in search of her.

At last, they met a great eagle who, from high in the sky, had seen the wicked demon Ravana taking Sita across the ocean to Lanka. So Rama, Lakshmana and Hanuman set off, south towards the sea.

When they got to the coast, Rama stood staring out across the water. There was no boat. It was too far to swim. So how was he ever going to reach his beloved Sita?

It was here that Hanuman used his magic power. He stood for a moment, catching his breath, and then with one great leap he jumped right across the sea and landed on the island of Lanka.

Quickly, he began his search for Sita. It was not long before he found her, inside Ravana's palace, in a courtyard, surrounded by high walls. Hanuman began to tell her all that had happened and how Rama would rescue her – but he was soon interrupted. For a demon can smell out a monkey and so Ravana was quickly on the scene.

But, as I said, Hanuman was no ordinary monkey and not at all afraid of Ravana. Boldly, he told the demon that if he didn't let Sita go free, Rama would bring an army to fight against Ravana.

That made Ravana roar with laughter. 'Take this foolish monkey outside,' he told his guards. 'And to teach him a lesson, set his tail on fire.'

The men did as they were ordered but Hanuman (who felt no pain) simply ran up a palm tree in the palace garden, setting the tree on fire as he climbed. From the top of that tree, he leapt to another, and to another, setting each one alight. And in all the smoke and confusion, Hanuman was able to escape, back to the edge of the sea. And there, with a second huge jump, he landed back on the mainland at the feet of Rama.

A great army of forest animals now came to their aid. Using the stones and pebbles from the beach, they built a great roadway out across the sea towards Lanka – and before too long a time had passed, they were able to reach the island.

There was the most terrible battle. On one side was Rama, Lakshmana, Hanuman and the forest army; and on the other side, all Ravana's demon guards. ☛

The battle went on for days until Ravana himself decided he must join the fighting. He started shooting poisoned arrows at Rama. Rama danced out of the way of some, and used his shield to protect himself from others. In return, he shot arrows at Ravana but none seemed to hurt the demon.

Then Rama decided he must use his holy power. Saying a prayer, he took a special arrow from his side, fitted it to his bow and took aim. Through the sky it flew, an arrow made of silver light. Its path was straight; its flight was fast and – as if it was not just a flash of silver but a terrible thunderbolt – it hit Ravana in the heart.

Down the demon fell. With a thud he hit the ground – and there he died.

In a second, Rama was in the palace; in another second he was in the courtyard; in a third, Sita was in his arms.

Without delay, they crossed the sea and made their way back towards the beautiful city of Ayodhya – for now, the fourteen years had passed and Rama was free to come home as King, with Sita as his queen.

By the time they reached the outskirts of Ayodhya, it was getting dark – but one woman saw them coming and lit a lamp. She placed it in her window to celebrate their home-coming and so that they might see their way. Her neighbour lit another lamp. A third, a fourth, a fifth; they all placed little lamps in their windows and soon the way was bright with flickering lights, celebrating the return of good King Rama.

And every year at Divali, Hindus light lamps to remember how Rama and his faithful friend, Hanuman, triumphed over wickedness and brought Sita safely home to Ayodhya. ◆

36

Confucius and friends

'Confucius' is a Latinized version of K'ung Fu-tzu (551–479BCE). Little is known for certain about this great Chinese philosopher but, after some years of manual labour, he became an accountant or court official and then a teacher. During a period of civil war, he fled to a neighbouring province and his influence began to spread. While Confucianism has always been regarded as the major Chinese religion, Confucius was not a religious leader but a teacher of ethics and morals. This story contains some of his sayings on these topics.

Some people say he was tall and very dignified. Others say he had big ears and sticking-out front teeth. And some people say he was a fussy, niggling, old-fashioned sort of person. The thing is, we don't really know what he looked like. He lived many hundreds of years ago, in China. He was called K'ung Fu-tzu but we know him as Confucius.

What we do know is that his friends wrote down a lot of the things that he said, and from these sayings we can tell that he was kind and generous; he liked making jokes, going swimming and playing other sports.

But Confucius was not always popular – as we shall see.

◆

AT FIRST, THERE were no problems. This was when his job was looking after some sheep and cattle. As he said, 'All I have to do is to see that the sheep and cattle grow up to be strong and healthy.' And because he was good at his job, they did.

But because he was good at that job, he was made a special adviser to Duke Ai, who was ruler of that part of China, which was called Lu. Confucius planned the building of new roads and bridges, he started schools and established a fair system of ☞

justice. One day, Duke Ai asked him, 'What else must I do to make the people respect me?'

'If you promote the good people over the bad, you'll be respected. But if you let the bad take advantage of the good, then you won't be respected.'

And this is where the trouble began. In those days, the powerful people of China were not always good. They loved showing off, strutting about in embroidered garments. In winter they wore lambswool and fox furs and the skins of rare animals. They collected jewels and pieces of jade, which is a precious, bluish-green stone. They rode in expensive carriages, decorated with bronze and brass and pulled by fine horses. And the poor people had to work hard to pay for all this extravagance. When Confucius pointed this out to the duke, the powerful people became jealous. As they said to each other, 'Who does this Confucius think he is? He used to be just been an ordinary shepherd and cowherd.'

'Confucius,' they said to each other, 'Confucius must go.' And Confucius, who was of course very wise, knew what they were thinking. So Confucius went.

He went before anybody could do anything to harm him. But he didn't go alone. He set off with a few friends, travelling in a little procession of very simple carriages. He was hoping to find a ruler wise enough to listen to his teachings. And at last he and his friends came to a part of the country called Wei, which was ruled by Duke Ling. There, Confucius started teaching. He taught ordinary, everyday things: 'Don't eat food that hasn't been properly prepared or which has gone bad. Don't eat except at meal times. Eat wisely, eat slowly.' And he taught other things. 'What you do not like being done to you, don't do to others.'

But Duke Ling of Wei was a cunning man. He'd been wanting to attack a neighbouring city and knew that Confucius was wise and clever. So Duke Ling asked Confucius about the best ways of leading an attack.

'I've never studied the matter of commanding troops,' said Confucius; and the next day, he and his friends decided it would be a good idea to leave that place as he didn't want to get involved in someone else's fighting.

They travelled on. Various people that Confucius had annoyed were looking for him by now, so he and his friends travelled in disguise, riding in simple farm carts. But Confucius was still hoping to find just one ruler who would pay attention to what he had to say about being good and kind to others.

One day, he met a hermit; a man who wants nothing to do with other people and who hides away, keeping himself to himself. The hermit listened to Confucius. 'Huh,' he said. 'You're wasting your time. People are mean. People are cruel. You're wasting your time, trying to teach them to be good. You must be stupid.'

Sadly, Confucius and his friends went on their way again. 'Why didn't you tell him he was wrong?' asked his friends.

'Not to mind when people are rude to you, that's the wise way,' said Confucius.

In the next village, they met a woman who was crying bitterly. 'What's the matter?' asked Confucius. She told him how her husband, uncle and son had all been killed by a tiger (for tigers lived in that part of China in those days). 'Why don't you move away, to a safe district?'

'Ah,' she said, 'but here we have a good ruler. I wouldn't move to where there's a bad government.'

'You see,' said Confucius to his friends, 'bad government is worse than a tiger.'

Soon after this, men came looking for Confucius, bringing presents. Duke Ai of Lu had realised how wrong he'd been and how wise Confucius was and now he wanted Confucius to return home. Confucius thought for a minute and then said, 'Yes, let's go home.' And so, happily, they went back to Lu and there his friends wrote down the sayings of wise old Confucius. And one of them, Tseng Tzu, wrote down what he had learned about how to be a good friend: 'Every night, I ask myself three things. In what I have done for others today, have I done my best? To my friends, have I been loyal and true? And have I told others to do only what I would do myself? If so, I've been a good friend.' ◆

37

The Buddha

Buddhism began in northern India. Its founder was a Hindu prince called Siddhartha Gautama who lived from about 560 to 480BCE. His father tried to protect him from any knowledge of suffering by keeping him inside the royal palace. Once Siddhartha understood the realities of life, he became a wandering hermit. Eventually, in his search for the meaning of life, understanding was granted him and he became the Buddha, 'the enlightened one'. He rejected the austere life of the ascetic and preached 'the middle way'.

Just suppose you were offered everything you ever wanted: money, your favourite meals and drinks, no work, no jobs, servants to do everything for you. You could have whatever presents you wanted whenever you asked for them. You would never hear about anything sad or miserable. But all this would have to be on one condition. You would have to stay in the same building for ever. Would the bargain be worth it?

Hundreds of years ago, this was what faced Prince Siddhartha Gautama. His father gave *him* everything he wanted – but kept him shut inside the royal palace. So was the prince satisfied? And would you be?

◆

IT WAS A beautiful palace. Of that there was no doubt. And the prince had everything he wanted. Cooling drinks. Delicious food. Servants to do everything he wished. And when he was bored, he played chess (which he enjoyed) or listened to music. But even so, Siddhartha was restless. It was all very well for the king, his father, to give him everything he wanted – but the palace was a prison. It was comfortable, yes; it was ☞

splendid. It had courtyards and fountains, gardens and fine decorations. As the Prince said, 'This palace is a paradise. The rooms are as brilliant as rain clouds in autumn. But I do wish I could make a journey outside the palace, to see what the world is really like.'

And after some time, he decided that he must see what was outside the palace. Eventually the king agreed and arranged an excursion, worthy of his son's dignity.

Siddhartha travelled by royal chariot; and, as he travelled, he questioned the royal charioteer.

'Charioteer, the people cheer me, do they not?'

'Indeed they do, my lord,' replied the royal servant.

But then the Prince noticed something he'd never seen before: a very old man, with a wrinkled face and bent back, bent almost nose to knee. 'That man there. What's the matter with him?' he asked.

'He's old my lord,' said the charioteer. 'That's all.'

'All?' said the prince, in dismay.

'Old age does that to everyone.'

'I did not realize… That is how age destroys beauty and youth and strength?'

'That is indeed the case.'

The prince then commanded the charioteer to drive back to the palace, at once. 'How can I delight,' he asked, 'in such a journey when my heart is afraid of old age?'

But nevertheless, the next day, the prince insisted on making another journey. Once again, the prince's attention was attracted by a person at the roadside.

'There, beside the road. What's the matter with that man?'

'That, my lord, is a leper.'

'Is that what people call disease?'

'That is what disease can do to a man.'

'Will I become ill one day?'

'No-one can escape illness any more than they can escape old age.'

Depressed, the prince returned to the palace. But yet again he determined to make another journey. The prince hoped very much to see no more suffering.

But this time he saw a group of men weeping, as they carried the dead body of their friend.

'What's that? What are those men carrying?' he asked.

'That, my lord,' said the charioteer, 'is a corpse.'

'Is that what happens to us all in the end?'

The charioteer nodded silently.

The prince was so saddened that he had no joy left in the fine things that surrounded him in the royal palace. And that night, he decided to give up his wealth, his jewels, his rich clothes and to live as a wandering hermit, trying to understand why there should be suffering in the world.

For the next five years, he wandered the countryside. He lived very simply, eating as little as possible – just a mouthful of pea soup or a handful of grain. Not surprisingly, he became very thin.

One day, in his search to understand what life was all about, what it was for, he came to a great fig tree called a bodhi tree. ☛

'I shall sit beneath this tree and though my flesh and bones may waste away and my life-blood dry, I shall not stir again until I have found the truth,' he said.

And as Siddhartha Gautama sat under that bodhi tree, the 'Truth' was revealed to him. From that time onwards, he was known as the Buddha, the enlightened one. He travelled the country with a new purpose, teaching what he now knew was the 'Truth'. He explained it like this:

'When we're full of selfish wants, we do not know what the world is really like. Put aside your desires and when you've lost your greed and selfishness, you'll see things as they really are, and that is happiness and freedom.

Think how you can be of use to the world; speak the truth; be straightforward in your actions; choose a job which isn't harmful to others; and take care of everybody and everything you meet.'

And the Buddha spent the rest of his life teaching and helping people – and spreading that wise message. ◆

38

The most precious merchandise

This Jewish story, retold from Jewish holy writings, emphasises the importance to believers of holy scripture and the importance of knowing what is of genuine value.

This is a story told by Jewish people about a merchant who went on a journey. It's also a story about something extremely precious and valuable: something more precious and valuable than gold and jewels. But what's that? Listen!

◆

A LONG, LONG time ago, a great sailing ship was getting ready to leave port for a distant country. While many wealthy merchants were going on board, all the valuable things they hoped to sell in that country were being loaded into the ship's hold, down below deck. There were clothes made of the finest silk, jewels, gold and silver and many, many cases of expensive wine.

Among the passengers on the ship was a stranger; a man the other merchants did not know.

'And what do you trade in?' they asked. 'What merchandise do you bring?'

'The most precious in the world.'

'What's that?' they all asked. But he'd say nothing more.

So they went below deck to see if they could discover what he'd brought on board. They checked every package and every packing case – but all they could find were their own cases. When they realized the stranger had no baggage at all, they

☞

began to laugh among themselves. 'He's not a proper merchant. He's brought nothing to sell!'

Soon they set sail. After several days at sea, a great storm arose and the ship was badly damaged. The sails were torn to ribbons, the mast broken and soon they were drifting helplessly towards some jagged rocks. There was nothing they could do to prevent the shipwreck. With a great crash the wind drove the ship onto the rocks; and there it stuck fast. The passengers and crew were able to scramble ashore but the wind and waves attacked what remained of the ship. Soon its timbers were beaten to splinters and all the cargo was lost, washed back out to sea. All the merchants' gold and silver and jewels: everything was lost.

As it turned out, they had reached the coast of the country to which they had been sailing. They were able to make their way on foot to the city where they had hoped to sell their goods. But instead of arriving with plenty of merchandise to sell, the merchants came empty-handed. Instead of being wealthy, they had to beg. Beg for food and beg for somewhere to sleep. But the stranger among them, well, he went to the local synagogue and asked to speak to the congregation. What he said proved he was a very learned man – and indeed it turned out that he had spent his whole life studying the Torah, the first five books of the Bible.

The people of the synagogue were greatly honoured to have such a person among them and so they asked him to stay with them. They also asked him to teach regularly in the synagogue and paid him to teach in a local academy or college. Many people came to listen to him as he explained the Torah. After several weeks though, the time came for him to return home. The people were sad to see him go but they gave him many presents.

Now, the merchants (who were still begging in order to stay alive) heard all this and they were astonished that such a man could be so popular. They went to him privately and asked if he could help them to return to their home country.

He told the people of the synagogue what the merchants wanted. The people said they would pay for the merchants to travel home on the same ship as the teacher – because such a learned man had asked for help on their behalf. And so the merchants and the teacher all went on board ship together – and as they put out to sea, the teacher said to the merchants, 'You thought I brought nothing with me. No merchandise. But I did. I brought something really valuable. I brought *knowledge*. The knowledge and teaching of God. That is something more precious than any jewels or silver or gold.'

And the merchants were silent because they knew now that this was so.

'Rabbi,' said one of them, 'you speak true. Yours *is* the most precious merchandise.' ◆

39

Ibrahim and the Ka'bah

For Jews, Abraham is one of the founding fathers or 'patriarchs' of their nation and religion. For them, his descendants are the 'Children of Israel'. (The name Abraham means 'father of many'.) The story of how God tested Abraham's obedience by asking him to sacrifice his son Isaac is told in Genesis chapter 22.

Ibrahim is the Arabic version of the word Abraham. Along with Moses, Ibrahim is the most frequently mentioned Prophet in the Qur'an. The Qur'an tells Muslims that Ibrahim rejected the worship of the sun, moon and stars and turned to the one creator God. This story of Ibrahim (who is also said to have rebuilt the Ka'bah in Makkah, or Mecca) is retold from the Muslim tradition (in which Ibrahim's first-born son is called Isma'il).

For Muslims, the most important building in the whole world is the Ka'bah in the city of Makkah. The word means 'cube' – and that is what it is. A granite building in the shape of a cube; twelve metres long, ten metres wide and fifteen metres high.

Muslims believe the first Ka'bah was built by the very first man, Adam. But that was long before the time of the man whom this story is about. Some people call him Abraham but Muslims know him as Ibrahim.

◆

ONE DAY, IBRAHIM had a dream in which God commanded him to sacrifice the life of his son Isma'il. He woke up with a start and looked at Isma'il who was sleeping nearby. What could be the meaning of this dream? And as he looked at the boy, he realized that his dream really *was* a command from God.

Because Ibrahim was obedient to God, he decided (with a

great sadness in his heart) that he must indeed kill his son. So Ibrahim and Isma'il set off towards a distant hillside. On their way, they met three men who each tried to persuade Ibrahim not to carry out the sacrifice – but Ibrahim remained faithful to what he thought was the will of God.

At last they reached the hillside which was near a place called Mina. Ibrahim tied up his son and put his hand on his sword. At that very moment, as Ibrahim was about to carry out the deed, he heard a voice. He turned round and saw a sheep caught in a bush. 'Ibrahim,' said the voice, 'kill this sheep in the place of Isma'il, for you have proved you are a loyal and faithful servant. I am well pleased with you.' And Ibrahim realized then that God had been testing him and had never wanted the death of Isma'il.

So Ibrahim sacrificed the sheep instead of his son – and father and son gave thanks to God.

Isma'il returned to live in Makkah – and every year Muslims all over the world still remember what is known as the Day of the Sacrifice.

Time went by and Ibrahim often prayed to God that he might be able to see his son Isma'il again. At last, God told him that he too should set off on the long and difficult journey to Makkah – and to build a House of God in that place.

As soon as Ibrahim arrived in Makkah, he got off his camel and went to a well called Zamzam. There was Isma'il. It was a joyful meeting. Ibrahim told his son what God had commanded him – and so they began work. Isma'il fetched stones from the nearby hills and Ibrahim laid them, to form a new Ka'bah or 'House of God'. They worked long and hard, each day from sunrise to sunset, and at last it was nearly completed. ☛

The very last stone which Ibrahim set in place was a special stone (said to have been brought from Heaven by the Angel Jibril, also known as Gabriel). It's still there, in the south-east corner of the Ka'bah.

When the work was finished, Ibrahim and Isma'il kissed that stone in praise of God. They were astonished to see that, when they kissed it, the stone shone with the love of God – because this was the very place where, long before all this, Adam had built the first Ka'bah.

That had happened after Adam had been sent away from the Garden of Eden where he had first lived with his wife Eve. After leaving Eden, Adam had travelled for a long time. Eventually he came to a place he believed was the centre point of all the land and there (as God had told him to do) he built the first Ka'bah as a house of praise to God.

But after the time of Adam, as the years went by, people forgot what the building was for. It was covered by sand and then destroyed by the Great Flood in the time of [Nuh] Noah.

But now Ibrahim and his son Isma'il had built a new Ka'bah in the very same place. This Ka'bah was kept holy for many years but, later, once again, people forgot what the building was meant to be used for.

Until, that is, many hundreds of years afterwards, when the last Prophet of Islam, the Prophet Muhammad, was yet again to make holy this special building as a place of worship to the One God – but that's another story.

Today, when Muslims make a holy journey or pilgrimage to the Ka'bah in Makkah, they know they are following not only in the footsteps of the Prophet Muhammad but in those of Adam – and especially of Ibrahim and his son Isma'il. ◆

40

The call of the Prophet

This is a retelling of the call of the Prophet Muhammad, the last Prophet of Islam. He lived in what is now Saudi Arabia circa 570–632CE and he received his 'call' and the revelation of the Qur'an from the Archangel Gabriel (or Jibril, as he is known in Arabic) in the year 610CE.

At this time, such religion as existed in that area was fairly primitive. There was also much fighting between families and local tribes, and oppression of the poor by the rich.

For Muslims, the followers of the religion Islam, the most important teacher of all time was the Prophet Muhammad who lived in a land called Arabia. This is the story of how he was called by God to start the religion of Islam.

◆

LONG AGO IN what we in the West call the sixth century, in a city called Makkah [which, you'll remember, was where Ibrahim had rebuilt the Ka'bah many years earlier], there lived a young man called Muhammad.

Both his parents had died before he was six and he'd been looked after by his grandfather and then, later, by an uncle. They were not wealthy: indeed, they were quite poor and Muhammad wasn't taught either to read or write and yet, when he was much older, God was to give him a book, a special book called the Holy Qur'an which Muhammad was to give to the world. But let's go back to when Muhammad was 20...

At this time, he was working for his uncle who lived in the city of Makkah and who bought and sold many things. And because Muhammad never tried to swindle their customers by overcharging them or by cheating on the weight of something, ☛

he became known as Al-Amin, which means 'the Trustworthy'. And that became his nickname.

One morning, his uncle sent for him. A wealthy widow called Khadijah (who also lived in Makkah) was looking for a young man to travel with (and care for) her camels which she sent to other cities, carrying the things that she was buying and selling.

Now Muhammad's uncle would have liked his nephew to stay and work for him in Makkah but, as he said, 'Business isn't so good. And Khadijah needs someone to help in *her* business. It's best if you work for her. If she'll give you the job, that is.'

So Muhammad went to her house. 'I'm looking,' she told him, 'for an honest young man who will take charge of my business. Your uncle has recommended you. So would you be interested in the job?'

Muhammad thought about it and then said yes. They talked about what he would have to do and soon everything was settled.

'I hear they call you Al-Amin,' she said. 'I hope that means you really *are* trustworthy.' Muhammad was a bit embarrassed but said he hoped he wouldn't let her down.

He worked hard and honestly and Khadijah's business began to do even better. She was very pleased with him. In fact she grew to like him very much – until one day she sent him a message. It was a proposal of marriage. From her to him. Again Muhammad thought it over – and then said yes.

The wedding took place and it proved to be a long and happy marriage.

Muhammad knew he was a fortunate man: he was happy, he was lucky. Even so, there were times when he felt almost suffocated with all the work and worry and business, with all the buying and selling. At times like this he wanted to feel close to God – so he would walk out of the city of Makkah, north to a hill called Mount Hira; and especially to one particular cave, high up in the mountain. There he could be alone and there he could think. And as he watched the beauty of the twilight and the stars and the moon, there in the cave of Hira, Muhammad knew the greatness of God, whom Muslims call Allah.

He began to spend more and more of his time at the cave, praying and thinking. Sometimes he stayed there for several days and Khadijah would send him food.

Now one particular night, when Muhammad was in the cave, he heard a voice. And there in front of him he saw a holy spirit, an angel. Muhammad looked in silence and wonder.

'Recite,' said the angel.

'What should I recite?' asked Muhammad. This happened three times and then the angel spoke again.

'Recite, in the name of Allah who made man from a drop of blood. Recite in the name of Allah.'

Muhammad repeated the words the angel spoke to him until he knew them by heart. Suddenly, the angel was gone and once again Muhammad was alone.

Quickly he made his way back down the mountainside to Makkah and to Khadijah. When he got home, he told her everything that had happened. 'Praise Allah,' she said.

For Khadijah had no doubt that Muhammad had been chosen to be a messenger for God, someone who would bring God's teaching to all the people. But Muhammad was doubtful. Why should God choose him for such a task?

Months passed. Many times Muhammad went back to the cave – and saw nothing. Then, ten months later, the angel appeared to him again. 'Warn the people. Tell them they must worship and praise Allah and give up their wicked ways and wrongdoing.'

After that, the angel (who was called Gabriel or Jibril) often appeared to Muhammad, giving him many more messages which he was to repeat to his family, to his friends and to any people of Makkah who would listen to what he had to say. And Muhammad taught them all the message of the angel – that there is only one God, whose name is God (or, as we have heard in Arabic, is Allah).

From then on, Muhammad was called the Prophet or God's Messenger; indeed he truly was Al-Amin, the Trustworthy. And all that the angel told him was written down in a book which can still be read today. It's called the Holy Qur'an and is treasured by all Muslims as the word of God. ◆

41

The Hijrah

Hijrah may be translated as 'departure', 'exodus' or 'flight'. It refers to the Prophet Muhammad's departure from Makkah (where he was facing increasing unpopularity) for Madinah. (Madinah was, in fact, called Yathrib until the Prophet's arrival there.)

The Muslim calendar dates from this event (16 July 622CE) and its anniversary is celebrated on each Islamic New Year's Day.

Sometime after the angel Jibril had revealed the teaching of the Holy Qur'an to the Prophet Muhammad, the Prophet started to teach the people of Makkah what had been told to him. Many people listened and believed and they became followers of this teaching, the way of Islam.

But there were plenty of people in Makkah who were cruel, selfish and even thuggish – and who worshipped false idols. They didn't welcome the Prophet's new message about the One God who wanted people to care for each other. So it was not surprising that Muhammad had his enemies.

◆

'HE'S NOT JUST a dreamer! He's dangerous!' One of the Prophet's enemies was losing his temper with the other rulers of the city of Makkah. 'Don't you see what'll happen? If he convinces the people that their idols are worthless and has them destroyed, who'll ever visit our city? We'll soon become poor.'

'Let's drive him out of the city,' shouted a second man.

'No, no. We mustn't let him leave the city,' replied a third called Abu Jahal.

☛

'Why's that?' asked yet another.

'Because he could go to the city of Madinah where he's even more popular, and he'll raise an army there to attack us. No. We must rid ourselves of him ... permanently!'

'Then let him be starved to death in his own house!' said another.

'That's it,' said the first speaker. 'We'll impose a ban that'll cut off all his sources of food.'

'And no-one shall trade with any of his family!'

For two years, the rulers of Makkah tried to impose their ban on the Prophet and his family – all to no effect. So they took a vote and decided to kill him outright.

That night, they arranged for Muhammad's house to be surrounded by twelve young men. But as these young men kept watch and as the night passed slowly, one by one, they became drowsy. Soon they were asleep.

Now God had warned the Prophet in a dream of what would happen and he had been keeping watch with his faithful friend Abu Bakr. When they saw the young men were asleep, they crept out of the house and the Prophet took some sand and sprinkled it over them. They slept on. They did not see Muhammad and Abu Bakr leave the city.

Knowing they would be expected to go north to Madinah, the Prophet and Abu Bakr decided to go south! Soon they came to the mountains which lie in that direction. They began climbing, searching for a place where they could hide in case their enemies did come that way. And at last, after scrambling up many steep paths, and over rocks and stones, they found a cave. A dark, lonely cave high up a hillside called Mount Thaur. And there they hid.

Meanwhile, back in the city of Makkah, the twelve men who were supposed to be guarding the Prophet's house were woken by a passing goatherd.

'What are you doing here?' he asked them.

'Waiting to kill Muhammad,' they muttered.

'But he's gone. I saw him go. He sprinkled some sand on you as he went. Look.'

When the rulers of Makkah found that the Prophet had escaped, they were furious. They set off in search of him, northwards towards Madinah. But soon they realized there were no tracks in the sand. They went back and hired an expert tracker to discover the route the Prophet had taken out of the city. A reward was offered: 100 camels for the man who captured Muhammad.

And it wasn't long before the Prophet's enemies were also climbing the mountains south of Makkah!

Inside the cave, the Prophet and Abu Bakr heard the noise of their enemies approaching. 'What can we do?' whispered Abu Bakr. 'There are just the two of us.'

'No,' said the Prophet. 'Three of us. Allah is with us. Don't worry.'

Outside, the tracker had found the mouth of the cave.

'They must be in there,' said one of the men who had come with him.

'No,' said the tracker. 'Look at the spiders' webs and the branches that cover its entrance. No-one's gone into that cave for months. We must move on.' And their voices became fainter and fainter as they moved away.

Abu Bakr moved cautiously to the front of the cave. Sure ☞

enough, across the mouth of the cave a spider had woven its web from one side to another. Above it, a branch hung low, weighed down by a grey dove which now was singing gently.

'How can this be?' asked Abu Bakr.

The Prophet smiled. 'Allah has made these things happen.'

For three or four days, the Prophet and Abu Bakr stayed hiding in the cave until Abu Bakr's son brought them camels to ride, and so they set off for Madinah, a slow and difficult journey of 300 miles across the desert. But, at last, look-outs in Madinah spied the two men approaching, and some of the crowds came out to welcome him at the nearby oasis called Quba. 'Our Prophet is here,' shouted the people. The Prophet returned their welcome and for three days he rested in Quba, accepting gifts of dates and honey. There he laid the foundation stone for the very first mosque (which is the name for a Muslim place of worship). Muhammad preached a sermon, the first he had given in safety and in the open air.

And then, in a joyful procession he went on into the city of Madinah. Amidst all the celebration, the Prophet called the procession to a halt. He dismounted, spread a cloth on the ground. Then he stood up and called aloud, 'Allah is most great'. And then he bowed his head to the ground and completed his prayer of thanksgiving.

And since then, these events have been remembered as Al Hijrah, the first day of the Muslim year. ◆

42

Visitors welcome

This is a retelling of a traditional Muslim story which illustrates the Eastern tradition of extending hospitality to travellers and visitors, known and unknown; and which teaches various lessons about generosity, politeness and the merit of not flaunting good works.

Suppose you've got just one small piece of chocolate. You're looking forward to eating it at break (or after school). And then a teacher says, 'Oh, do share it with so-and-so. They've no chocolate at all.' Would you keep it all for yourself? Or would you break it in even smaller pieces so you each had a tiny bit? Or would you give it all away? And if you did that, would you let on to the teacher or the other person that you were going without?

Now imagine that it's not a piece of chocolate you're being asked to share but all the food you've got to last you through the day and night.

This is a [another] story about the time of the Prophet Muhammad, the Prophet of Islam.

◆

IN THE DAYS when the Prophet Muhammad was living in Madinah, there came a poor traveller to the city. He was tired and weary from his journey across the desert and in need of food and somewhere to rest.

Now it so happened that, as he entered the city, he met the Prophet Muhammad himself, who was talking with some of his friends and followers.

'You are welcome, stranger,' said the Prophet to the man. Then the Prophet turned to the other Muslims who were ☞

there. 'You know our custom: we always offer food and hospitality to our guests – so who will invite this man to dinner?'

In those days, there were many poor people in the city of Madinah. They did not have enough money to buy food for themselves or their families and a number lived in houses that were broken and in need of repair. So even though they knew it was right and good to offer a visitor a meal and a place to rest, many of those who were standing there could not afford to do so.

It wasn't surprising then that no-one answered the Prophet's question. They stood awkwardly, looking at the ground. He asked the same thing again. This time, one man looked up. His name was Abu Talha.

'I'll invite him to dinner,' he said. 'He shall be my guest.' Then he turned to the traveller and bid him welcome. 'My new friend, you are welcome to my home tonight.'

The traveller was very pleased and accepted the invitation, so the two men walked together through the streets of Madinah until they came to the small, white stone house where Abu Talha lived. His wife met them at the door and Abu Talha told her that the visitor was to be their guest for dinner that evening.

Abu Talha's wife smiled and bowed and stood aside while Abu Talha led the visitor into the main room of the little house and signed that he should sit down and rest. Then he excused himself and went to the tiny back room where his wife prepared their meals.

'What is it?' he asked. 'You made our guest welcome with your smile but you did not smile with your eyes. What is your worry?'

'But my husband – what am I to do?'

Abu Talha was puzzled. 'Prepare a meal for us. That is usual when we have a guest.'

His wife sighed and nodded sadly.

'What's the matter? Is something wrong?' asked Abu Talha.

'It's so embarrassing,' she said. 'I've only enough food in the house for our children. If that. I've nothing for us to eat at all. So what can I offer to a guest?'

'But I've given my promise to the Prophet that I'll be this man's host tonight.' And Abu Talha was now as worried as his wife. After a moment he said, 'Send the children to bed early.'

'But what about their supper?'

'Never mind. They can do without for just one night. Now this is what I want you to do.'

Then he told her his plan.

She sent the children to bed and told them to keep as quiet as possible. Then she cooked the small amount of food that was in the house. When it was ready, Abu Talha invited his guest to sit down to eat. But as he did, Abu Talha said, 'If you don't mind, I think perhaps we won't let the lamp burn so brightly. Your eyes must be tired from the desert sun. I'll just turn it down. It's nice to eat by candlelight.'

So he turned the oil-lamp down very low and lit just one candle which he placed in the far corner of the room. It was now so dark, you could hardly see across the table.

'You're eating too?' the traveller asked.

'Of course, of course,' replied Abu Talha. But his wife served food only to their guest, and then gave an empty dish and spoon to her husband and took one for herself. So when the ☞

meal began, only their guest was eating – although, in the gloom, you could hear three spoons busy in three dishes. For this had been Abu Talha's plan: to give their honoured guest all the food they had, and just pretend to eat themselves.

And it all worked out as he hoped. The visitor never realized what was happening because it was so dark in the room. If he'd known what was going on, he might have been upset – and that was not how Abu Talha wanted any guest to feel.

Indeed, their visitor was a very happy man when he left Abu Talha's house, thanking him and his wife for their goodness to a traveller. And Abu Talha and his wife were also happy. Hungry but happy. They had done a good deed; they had done what was polite and they had done what was expected of them. What's more, they had managed to keep their secret. And no-one ever knew just what it had cost them.

Except the next time Abu Talha met the Prophet, the Prophet smiled and said, 'Talha, Allah is pleased that you were prepared to sacrifice your needs for the sake of others.'

How much did he know? Had he guessed?

All Abu Talha said was, 'It was nothing. It was what anyone would have done.'

'No,' said the Prophet. 'It's *not* what anyone would have done. It's what everyone *should* have done.' ◆

43

The night journey

This story of an event also known as the 'Mi'raj' tells how Muhammad, the Prophet of Islam, was taken from Makkah on a miraculous journey to the temple in Jerusalem. He was guided by the Archangel Jibril and travelled on a winged horse called Burraq. From the site where Solomon's temple once stood, Muhammad made a journey into heaven, meeting several of the prophets on his way. Besides being an important story within the religion of Islam, the Mi'raj points up many of the connections between three of the great world religions: Islam, Christianity and Judaism.

This is a [another] story about the Prophet Muhammad, the founder of the religion of Islam. One night he felt he was taken on a very strange and special journey from Makkah (the holy city where he lived) to Jerusalem. From Jerusalem he felt himself guided upwards into the presence of God in heaven.

As we'll hear, the Prophet Muhammad met other prophets who had been the leaders and teachers of other religions. And we'll also hear how he learned several of the teachings of Islam which are still kept today by those who follow that religion.

◆

IT WAS NIGHT-TIME in the holy city of Makkah. The Prophet Muhammad, tired after the heat and cares and general busyness of the day, slept deeply. It was a quiet, untroubled sleep.

Then, suddenly, he heard a voice calling him and he saw (standing by where he slept) the angel Jibril. Jibril was beckoning, beckoning the Prophet Muhammad to follow him. ☛

As if in a dream, Muhammad left his bed and followed the angel across the room and out through the doorway of the house. And there, waiting for them, was the most magnificent white horse. It was a mare, with a flowing white mane. But what was most remarkable was the fact that the horse had wings like those of an eagle – but even larger.

'This is Burraq,' said Jibril. And together they mounted Burraq and immediately the horse was flying; flying higher and higher through the cool night air – and the city of Makkah was soon left far behind.

Before long, Jibril told Burraq to descend from the night sky, back down to earth – and as she did, Muhammad saw that they had arrived at another holy city, the city of Jerusalem. In just a short while, they had completed a journey that would have taken many days or even weeks had they travelled by land.

Burraq landed gently at the temple that was in that city, and Muhammad tied the horse to a ring on the wall, as was the custom in those days. And then Jibril led Muhammad into the temple and there they met Moses and Jesus (whom Muslims call Musa and Isa) and holy men from other times – and they prayed there together.

Then, on leaving the temple, Jibril offered Muhammad a drink. A drink of either milk or wine. Muhammad chose milk. 'You have chosen rightly,' said Jibril. 'From now on, Muslim people will not drink alcohol lest it confuses their minds and they go astray and do wrong.'

It was then that Muhammad saw another wondrous thing: a ladder, seemingly made out of light, leading up into heaven. And Jibril motioned to Muhammad that they should climb the ladder – and in this way Muhammad entered heaven. There he met Adam who had been the first man on earth; and next he met Noah [Nuh] and again he met Moses and Jesus and other prophets, including Aaron the brother of Moses and John the Baptist who was cousin to Jesus.

At last, Muhammad came to the very highest part of heaven where the Tree of Heaven grows; and it was here that he was given all the laws of the Muslim religion which is called Islam – a word which means 'giving yourself up to do God's will'.

On his way back down to earth, Muhammad again met Moses. 'How often a day must followers of your religion say their prayers?' asked Moses.

'Fifty, I was told,' said Muhammad.

'That's too many. No-one will remember to pray fifty times a day!' said Moses.

So Muhammad returned to the highest part of heaven to ask for a smaller number. And, again, on his way back down he met Moses once more.

'How many prayers are now ordered?' he asked.

'Forty.'

'That's still too many!' said Moses.

Muhammad went back several times until the number of prayer times was reduced to five.

'That's still too many,' said Moses.

'I'd be ashamed to return again,' said Muhammad and that is why Muslims say prayers to God five times each day.

Muhammad then continued his way back to earth, down the ladder. And, at the foot of it, Jibril and Muhammad found Burraq still waiting. Muhammad untied her and they climbed on her back and returned quickly to Makkah, through the ☛

night air, to the very house where Jibril had found Muhammad sleeping. They arrived at the very moment that the first rays of sunlight announced the start of a new day. The Prophet Muhammad's night journey to Jerusalem and to heaven above had taken just a short while.

It was many years later that Muslims built a special place of worship in Jerusalem as a reminder of that night journey. It was a holy building, a mosque called the Dome of the Rock and it still stands on the very spot where, it is said, Muhammad climbed the ladder to heaven. What is more, it is the same spot where, centuries before, King Solomon had built his temple, also to the glory of God. ◆

44

Suleman the Humble

This is a retelling of a Muslim story which teaches the dangers of self-importance and pride, and the virtue in helping others. (It is worth noting that not all the details of this traditional story agree with the history of Madinah at this time.)

I wonder if you've ever met anyone who thinks they're very important. Even if they're not. They say things like, 'I should have first go, 'cause I'm older than you.' Or, 'You've got to do what I say, because I'm bigger than you.' Perhaps they think a lot of themselves because they're good at something – or maybe they don't like doing ordinary things for themselves. 'Carry this for me,' they say. 'I'm important, I don't have to carry things for myself.'

Well, this is a story about someone who really was important. He was called Suleman and he lived a long, long time ago in the time of Muhammad who was the last prophet of the religion of Islam.

◆

SULEMAN WAS IMPORTANT. In fact, he was a very important person in the city of Madinah – because he was the ruler of Madinah.

Now although Madinah was called a city, in those days it wasn't at all like a modern city. For a start, it was in the middle of the desert but it did have a spring which meant there was a supply of water, and trees grew there, so there was shade. It was an important place for travellers who could stay and rest there [as we heard before].

One traveller who had come to Madinah was the Prophet ☞

167

Muhammad himself [when he had to escape from men who had become his enemies in Makkah]. And when Muhammad came to Madinah, Suleman had listened to the message that Muhammad brought from God, whom Muslims call Allah. He listened, and listened. And as he knew that what Muhammad was saying was true, he became one of Muhammad's friends or companions. And he also went on being ruler of Madinah.

But you'd never have thought so. He lived in a simple house. He was richer than some of the people of Madinah [such as Abu Talha] and, yes, he had servants but no more than he needed and he treated them very fairly. He never said, 'I'm important, you must do what I say.'

And if you'd met him in the street, you'd never have guessed who he was. You'd have never have said, 'This is the ruler of Madinah.'

Now, one particular day, just as Muhammad had once come travelling across the desert to Madinah, so another visitor came to the city. Like many of the people of those times and of that region, he was a merchant who travelled across the desert from town to town, selling things, and he had many camels to carry all the things he bought and sold.

So, as I said, he came to Madinah (with his camels) and the first person he met was Suleman. Suleman was walking along, all on his own because he hadn't liked to bother a servant to saddle up one of *his* camels just so that he could take a look round his city. And of course the merchant had no idea who he was. He called out to him. 'Oi! You! Come here!'

Now Suleman might have taken no notice and gone on his way or he might have said, 'Don't you know who I am?' But he didn't do either of these things.

He came over to the merchant.

'*Assalam-o-Alaikum*,' he said which was the greeting they said in that place. 'Peace be with you,' it means.

But all the merchant said was, 'Look, I've got a bale of straw. That big bundle there. On the first camel. It's for someone who lives in this place and it needs delivering, so you can carry it! I'm far too important to start carrying bundles of straw around. I'm a merchant.'

Suleman said nothing.

'Look here,' said the merchant, bossily. 'You stand with your back to the camel. I'll untie the bundle, lower it onto your shoulders and then you can carry it the rest of the way. Now look sharp.'

And that's what Suleman did. Without a word, he took the weight of all the straw onto his shoulders – and struggled off down the street, with the merchant walking proudly behind him. It was a very heavy bundle.

'Hurry up. You're dawdling,' said the merchant as Suleman began to go more slowly. So Suleman hurried up as best he could. And then, coming towards them came another man (who lived in Madinah). As this man approached them, he recognized Suleman and greeted him '*Assalam-o-Alaikum*,' he said (which, as I told you, means 'Peace be with you.') And he bowed very low and very respectfully to Suleman. And from under the bale of straw and a bit out of breath, Suleman said, '*Wa Alaikum salam*!' which means 'And peace be with you, too.'

Well, the man was about to go on his way but the merchant stopped him.

'Aren't you going to greet *me* as well?' he said, very pompously.

'Oh yes. *Assalam-o-Alaikum*,' said the man and started to go on his way again.

'Wait a minute,' said the merchant.

'Yes?' said the man.

'Aren't you going to bow to me? Why don't you bow to me, as you did to this, this ... person?'

'Oh!' said the man. 'Well, no. No. I bow only to the ruler of the city of Madinah.'

'Very well,' said the merchant, rather crossly. 'Off you — You what? You bow only to ... You mean this man who's carrying my bale of straw is the ... the ruler of this city?'

'Yes, he's Suleman, whom we call Suleman the Humble.'

'But he said nothing ... I asked him if he'd mind carrying ... Well, I suppose I did actually rather *tell* him to ... Look, my dear sir,' he said to Suleman. 'I apologize. And I must carry my own bale of straw.'

'No,' said Suleman. 'You're a visitor. I will honour a visitor to our city and I won't put the bale down till we've reached the house where you're going.'

'But you're an important person.'

'An important person can do things for other people. Just as we can all think of other people. You see, my friend — I may call you my friend? Yes, my friend ... Some people happen to be rulers of cities. Some happen to be very strong. Or very clever. Or very patient. Or humble. Or ... whatever. That's the will of Allah. It's no reason to boast. And no reason not to care for those they meet.'

And as you can guess, everyone liked Suleman because he followed the way of God and his Prophet Muhammad, and also because he was good and kind – and not proud, even though he was important. ◆

45

The sacred thread, the amazing prayer and Guru Nanak's feet

The first teacher or 'Guru' of Sikhism was Guru Nanak. He was born into a Hindu family in 1469CE in a village called Talwandi in what is now Pakistan. The people in that area were either Hindus or Muslims. Nanak rejected the Hindu caste system and stressed the equality of all men and women. He also rejected aspects of the other major religion of that area, Islam – such as the Islamic injunction on its followers to face Makkah when praying.

Guru Nanak's birthday is observed in late November.
NB It may not be appropriate to use this story where Guru Nanak's criticisms of Hindu and Muslim practices may cause confusion and worry for young Hindus and Muslims.

Many years ago, in fact more than 500 years ago, there lived in India a boy called Nanak; a very wise young boy. So wise was he that there came a time when his teachers said there was nothing left to teach him. When he grew up, he became the first leader of one of the great religions of the world, Sikhism. But this story begins when Nanak was still a young boy and, even if everyone thought he was wise and clever, not everyone thought he was good.

◆

IT ALL BEGAN when Nanak's father (who was called Kalu) thought Nanak was making bad friends, especially at school. So Kalu decided to get a teacher to come and teach Nanak at home and, because the family were all Hindus, Kalu chose a Hindu as a teacher for his son.

When Hindu boys are growing up, usually some time between their seventh and twelfth birthdays, their teacher or a Hindu priest puts a thread around their neck. The thread is in the shape of a loop and is usually red or yellow or white. It's a sign that the boy is now grown up and must be 'responsible' for himself. That is, it's now his own duty to see that he says his prayers properly, that he treats holy men and holy books with respect; and that he honours his parents, and cares for old people, the poor and animals.

Of course, all this takes a lot of effort and concentration – but some people (including Nanak's new teacher) believed that, just by wearing the thread, you would automatically become good! They believed the thread itself would make a boy behave well.

So the time came when this teacher made a thread for Nanak, and then tried to put it round his neck. Nanak (who, you remember, was a very wise boy) had a question for him.

'Please,' said Nanak, 'please wait. I want to understand why you're putting the thread round my neck.'

'It'll make you a good boy,' said the teacher. 'God'll see it and then He'll love you.'

'But how can a thread make me good? Wearing a thread won't make me good – and how can God love me if I don't do good?'

'Oh, you're just a child,' said the teacher. 'You don't understand. Put it on.'

'But what if it breaks when I have my bath?' asked Nanak. 'How will God see it then?' And as his teacher couldn't answer that, he became rather cross.

There are many other stories told about Nanak, about when he was young, and also about when he was older and went about the country as a teacher himself – by which time he was ☛

known as Guru Nanak (because the word 'Guru' means 'teacher').

There was, for example, the time when Guru Nanak and a friend called Mardana were on a journey. They came to a village where everybody was rude and unkind to them. Guru Nanak and Mardana were given nothing to eat and they had to sleep in the open air.

Even so, next morning, before they left, Guru Nanak blessed the village and prayed that all the people there would stay safely in that village for ever and ever – which surprised Mardana, but he said nothing, and they went on their way.

That evening, they came to another village where everything was totally different. Nanak and Mardana were well looked after. They were given splendid food and they were offered very comfortable beds in which to sleep. In the morning, Guru Nanak blessed the people – and prayed that they would be scattered all over the world.

Mardana couldn't keep quiet this time.

'That's amazing. Why did you say that prayer?'

'Well,' said the Guru, 'wherever the good people of this village go, they'll do good and make other people good. And the bad and mean people from where we were last night, well, it's far better for everyone if they stay together, where they are.'

Guru Nanak taught many other things: that men and women are equal and should be treated equally. He taught that we should work hard and help others – and that there is only one God and that he is everywhere.

There was a time when Guru Nanak made this quite clear. He had made a journey to the Muslim holy city of Makkah and he was very tired after his long journey so he lay down in the open air to rest. By chance, his feet were pointing towards the Muslim holy building, the Ka'bah, where Muslims worship God. A Muslim man called Rukandin was nearby and he, like all Muslims, faced Makkah and the Ka'bah whenever he said his prayers. He was horrified by what Nanak was doing.

'It's a great insult. You're pointing your dirty feet towards the holy house of God. It's most disrespectful.'

'Oh,' said Guru Nanak. 'I thought God was everywhere. Would you please turn me round so my feet are pointing in any direction where God is not present.'

Rukandin tried moving him round but Nanak stopped him. 'God doesn't live in one place. He is everywhere.' ◆

46

Guru Nanak and the banquet

This is another story about the first teacher of Sikhism, Guru Nanak (see the previous story). Its message is that we are all of equal value in the sight of God. It is also a warning against having too high an opinion of oneself.
NB The sound '-ji' [say: 'jee'] after a name or title is a mark of respect.

Who's the more important: a rich man or a poor man? Some people seem to think that being rich makes you more important or in some way 'better' than other people. But the man who started the Sikh religion about 500 years ago, Guru Nanak, thought not. He travelled around India and what is now Pakistan teaching people how God wanted them to be kind to each other and to be honest and truthful.

And one of the things he taught was that all men and women are equally important and that it is what you do that makes you good or bad.

◆

ONE OF THE cities Guru Nanak visited was Eminabad, in part of the country called the Punjab. While Guru Nanak was in Eminabad, many people came to listen to him because he was such a wise and holy man. One of those who heard him was a very poor carpenter called Lalo.

When Guru Nanak had finished talking for the day, Lalo went shyly up to him.

'Guru-ji,' he said. 'I'm only a poor man and you're a great and wise man, but you're a traveller and a visitor to our city and I should like to offer you a meal tonight.'

'Lalo, *you* are a kind and generous man,' replied Guru Nanak, 'and I'll be delighted to accept.'

'But you must know that I can't offer much. Some water to drink and vegetables and rice, that's all. And a little bread perhaps.'

'That'll be excellent, for that's all I need and all I want. I'm truly delighted to accept your invitation.'

And so they walked back together, through the crowded streets, to the little house where Lalo lived.

Now in another part of the city, there lived a very rich businessman called Malik Bhago. He hadn't bothered to go and listen to Guru Nanak: he'd been much too busy making deals that were to his advantage. But he'd heard talk of how Guru Nanak was a respected and very popular person.

'I'll invite him to dinner,' said Malik Bhago to himself. 'And when he comes, that'll prove to everyone in the city that I'm just as generous and good as he is.'

Which of course he wasn't. Not only was he cruel to his workers, he was unfair and he was mean. But he was rich and powerful – so everyone had to do what he said. And when he told his servants to find Guru Nanak and invite him to dinner that evening, that is what they did. At once, double quick.

They looked everywhere. But they never thought of looking in the house of someone like Lalo. As they searched the streets of the city, they asked everyone they met: 'Have you seen Guru Nanak? Which way did he go?'

At last they found someone who'd seen Guru Nanak going home with Lalo – so they raced round to Lalo's house. Double quick – because they knew that Malik Bhago's temper wouldn't be getting any better with all the waiting.

'Guru Nanak,' they said as soon they'd found him, 'you must come to Malik Bhago's house at once. You're invited to dinner.'

'Must?' asked Guru Nanak.

'Everyone does what Malik Bhago says,' said Lalo very quietly. 'And you'll get a very much better meal.'

'No,' said Guru Nanak. 'I'll stay here. I was glad to accept Lalo's kind invitation.'

'But you don't understand,' said Malik Bhago's servants. 'Our master'll be furious if you refuse him.'

'And he does always have a splendid meal of freshly cooked delicacies,' added another.

'I really think you should go,' said Lalo.

Guru Nanak was silent for a few moments.

'Very well,' he said at last. 'I'll go. But I'll take a piece of that bread you have baked, Bhai Lalo.'

Everyone looked amazed. Not because of what he'd said about the bread. What surprised them was that Guru Nanak called him 'Bhai Lalo' – for by doing that, he was paying him a great honour. 'Bhai' (which means 'Brother') is used only when you wish to pay someone a very great honour.

Malik Bhago's servants led Guru Nanak through the streets to his house, and when they got there, Malik Bhago invited Guru Nanak to sit down and then, very bossily, ordered his servants around.

Soon the meal was ready. And it really was a very special meal which had taken a lot of people a great deal of time to prepare and had cost more than Bhai Lalo would earn in a whole month.

But just as they were about to eat, Guru Nanak took two pieces of bread, one in each hand. One was the one that Bhai Lalo had baked and the other was from Malik Bhago's house.

And Guru Nanak did a very strange thing. He squeezed both pieces of bread. Out of the bread that Bhai Lalo had baked dripped pure fresh milk – and out of the bread from Malik Bhago's house there came drops of blood.

'What does this mean?' asked Malik Bhago.

'It means,' said Guru Nanak, 'that I'd prefer to eat Bhai Lalo's plain food which has been earned by his hard work and pre- pared with care by himself – rather than eat this banquet which has been made possible only because you've become rich by cheating the poor and by tricking those with whom you do business.'

And as Malik Bhago watched the last drops of blood trickle from his piece of bread, he was very quiet. 'I think,' he said after a while, 'I think that tomorrow I'll come to hear you teach. I think I've made —,' he hesitated. 'I think I've made mistakes in the past. I think I must — I must —'

'Be kinder to other people?' suggested Guru Nanak.

'Exactly what I was going to say.'

'And what you will do. I hope,' said Guru Nanak.

'I'll try.'

'And you'll invite Bhai Lalo to supper?'

'Lalo? To supper? But he's just —'

'To God, a poor person is just as important as a rich person.'

Malik Bhago was silent.

'So you *will* ask him to supper?' ◆

47

The boy who became a Guru

The ten Gurus of Sikhism led their community for more than 200 years from its foundation by Guru Nanak until the death of the tenth Guru, Guru Gobind Singh in 1708CE. Each was chosen by his predecessor for his abilities as a teacher and guide. Guru Gobind Singh (the son of the ninth Guru) did not nominate a successor: instead the book which contained the hymns of the Gurus, the Guru Granth Sahib, was to be the Sikhs' teacher and guide – as it still is.

As a boy, Guru Gobind Singh was known as Gobind Rai: Singh is a name or title meaning 'lion' which all male Sikhs have taken since his time.

This story shows how Gobind Rai learned (and taught) what is of real value – including religious toleration.

If you had two bangles or bracelets of pure gold, would you take care of them? This is the story of a boy who had two such bangles – and who threw them away. He was a Sikh who grew up to be the teacher or leader of all the Sikhs: their 'Guru' [just as Guru Nanak had been, many years before]. His name was Guru Gobind Singh and he was to be the last of the ten great Gurus of the Sikh religion. Of course, when he was young, he wasn't called 'Guru': his name then was simply Gobind Rai – and this is his story.

◆

HIS FATHER WAS away from home and Gobind Rai was living with his mother in the Indian city of Patna – and, from time to time, he was not exactly well-behaved. When that happened, his mother had to get cross with him. But this particular day, when she called him in from playing with some other boys, she didn't have to pretend to be cross: she really was cross. 'Someone's been to see me today,' she said to Gobind Rai.

'That was good, wasn't it?' he said, smiling.

'No, Gobind Rai. It wasn't good. Indeed, she was very angry. With you.'

'Me, mother? What've I done wrong?'

'That's what I want you to tell me,' answered his mother. 'She said you'd been shooting at her.'

'Oh, *that* woman.'

'So it's true?'

Gobind Rai laughed. 'It was just a bit of fun. You see, I was with my friends and we'd been playing with my bow and arrows, aiming at a target, and then along came this woman carrying a water pot on her head and my friends all wanted to see if I could hit a moving target. And I could.'

'Your arrow broke the water jar,' said his mother sternly.

'She didn't get very wet.'

'It was thoughtless and cruel. And dangerous. You might have hit her.'

'But mother, you know I'm a good shot. There was no danger I'd miss the pot.'

Gobind Rai's mother was still cross. 'If you want to practise shooting at moving targets, then you should be brave enough to go into the forest and try your skill on lions and leopards!'

At that, Gobind Rai fell silent. But when he was older, he would be brave enough to go into the forest. In fact, he became a great soldier, as well as being a fine archer. Yet when he was a boy, he often surprised the people around him in other ways.

He used to wear two gold bangles on his wrist and one day, ☛

when he and his friends were playing by a river, throwing stones into the water, he took off one of the bangles and threw it into the water. Then he took off the other one and threw that into the river as well. Again, his mother was angry.

'Now, what did you do that for? They're gold!'

'Don't worry,' said Gobind Rai 'They're *only* gold. Remember what my father said.'

'What do you mean? "Only gold"?'

'You tell me to sing his hymns each day. You know what he wrote in one of them: "Whoever values gold no more than iron, no power on earth can make a slave." Well, I won't be a slave to gold. That's why I threw the bangles away. We don't want to spend our lives worrying about such things.'

It was soon after this that a letter came from his father asking the family to leave Patna and return to him, and to their homeland, the Punjab. Now, Gobind Rai's father was a very important man: he was the Guru or leader of all the Sikh people and his name was Guru Tegh Bahadur [*say:* taig b'harder]. [There had been other Gurus before him – beginning with Guru Nanak. Tegh Bahadur was the ninth Guru of Sikhism.]

Guru Tegh Bahadur was worried. The Emperor of India, Emperor Aurangzeb was trying to make the Hindu people of Kashmir become Muslims. He was forcing them to eat beef, which is forbidden for Hindus. And now many Hindus had come to Guru Tegh seeking his protection.

'Aurangzeb has offered them a choice,' he explained to Gobind Rai. 'They can become Muslims or they can die. Many have had their wives and daughters taken from them. Their houses have been burned to the ground.'

'That is not the Muslim way,' said Gobind Rai quietly.

'It's the way of Aurangzeb. The Emperor of India, my son, has lost his senses. Only some great sacrifice can stop his cruelty.'

Gobind Rai looked at his father. It was his turn to be worried. 'You have written: "If you wish to lend a helping hand, you might have to sacrifice yourself."'

Guru Tegh nodded but said nothing. Even so he went to Aurangzeb.

Some weeks later, a most brave Sikh, Bhai Jeewan came to Gobind Rai and his mother. He was most distressed at the news he had to bring. 'The Guru tried so hard, madam,' he said, blinking back his tears. 'He spoke so well. He argued, reasoned with Emperor Aurangzeb that what he was doing was wrong. But the Emperor wouldn't listen. He gave a choice to your husband; to your father, Gobind Rai.'

'Which was?' asked Gobind Rai, already fearing the answer.

'Become a Muslim. Or...'

'Or what?'

'Die.'

'My father would not give up his faith.'

'You're right,' said Bhai Jeewan. 'He was executed there and then. And Aurangzeb gave orders that his body should be left in the public square in the centre of Delhi as a warning to all who dare to challenge Aurangzeb.'

'Gobind Rai, my son —' began Gobind Rai's mother.

'I'm all right mother,' he interrupted her.

'You may cry. It wouldn't be childish to cry at such a time. Nor to be angry.'

'We must be calm, mother.'   ☛

Soon after that day, Gobind Rai was himself named as the next Guru and as the years went by, he taught his people the ways of their religion - and (when all else fails) the ways of making war to defend their faith.

But Guru Gobind never tried to make the Muslims and the Hindus into Sikhs as Emperor Aurangzeb had wanted to make all people into Muslims.

No, Guru Gobind wanted all men and women to be free - and equal. As he said, 'All men are the same, although they may look different. The fair-skinned and the dark; the ugly, the beautiful; the Hindu, the Muslim... All human beings have the same eyes, the same ears, the same body. All human beings are *reflections* of the one God.' ◆

48

The founding of the Khalsa

The 'Khalsa' is the brotherhood of all Sikh men and women. Its foundation dates from when Guru Gobind Rai, the tenth and last Guru (see the previous story) summoned the Sikhs to Anandpur. It is from that time that Sikh men have worn their 'uniform' of uncut hair (covered with a turban), comb, bracelet, shorts, and sword.

Sikhs celebrate this event each year (usually about 13 April) at the festival of Baisakhi – which is actually both a Hindu and Sikh festival.

Guru Gobind Rai led a man into the tent. A few minutes later, the Guru came out, his sword dripping with blood. 'Who's next?' he asked.

Well, would you volunteer? Would you go into that tent?

This happened one day in the year 1699 when Guru Gobind Rai (who [you'll remember] was the tenth of the Sikh 'Gurus' or teachers) [and who, by now, was a young man] called all the Sikhs together at a place called Anandpur and there he asked no less than five of them to follow him into that tent. It seemed he was asking them to make a most terrible sacrifice: to give up their lives. So what was it all about? What was the point of it all?

◆

IN INDIA, THE wheat and grain are ready for harvesting in the month called Baisakhi – which happens about the time of year when it's April in this country. But just before the Sikhs in India start the work of gathering in the crops, they have always met together for a festival.

And that was why, about 300 years ago, in the year 1699, Guru Gobind Rai had called all the Sikhs to meet him at Anandpur ☞

– or so everyone thought. They gathered in front of his tent, expecting that (as usual) there would be prayers and that they would sing some hymns. But after a while, the Guru came out of his tent, wearing a bright new saffron yellow tunic tied with a blue sash, and he also wore a turban to cover his hair. In his hand, he held a sword.

'This isn't how it usually is,' muttered one or two of the crowd who quickly became quiet as the Guru began to speak.

'By my sword,' said Guru Gobind Rai, 'I ask if there's one among you who will prove his faith by giving me … his head? Who will offer up his life?'

Now the Sikhs had plenty of enemies in India at that time and many of them feared they might be killed by their enemies but they never expected it would be one of their own leaders who would want to take their life.

Not surprisingly, there was a long silence. Then the Guru asked again, 'If there be any true Sikh here, let him offer up his head as proof of his faith.'

And from out of the crowd, a warrior Sikh from Lahore stepped forward. He was called Daya Ram and he spoke out bravely. 'My Guru and my lord. My humble head is yours, if so you wish it.'

The Guru led him into the tent. There was a moment's silence and then, from inside the tent, there came a dull thud. Then the Guru came out – with his sword which was now dripping blood. Immediately he spoke again. 'If there be another true Sikh, let him now offer me his head as proof of his faith.'

This time a very poor farmer, Dharam Das from Delhi, came forward. 'If it's your will, then I'll follow,' he murmured. Guru Gobind Rai led him into the tent. Again a thud was heard.

Again, the Guru reappeared with his sword dripping blood. And once again he asked for the head of a Sikh.

This time it was a poor washerman from Gujerat, a man called Mukham Chand, who volunteered. He too was led into the tent; a thud was heard and the Guru reappeared with his sword now bloodier than ever.

Not surprisingly, some of the crowd had begun to edge quietly away, just in case anyone should suggest they were next. But what was surprising was that a fourth and fifth Sikh stepped forward when the Guru asked for yet more men to offer up their lives to prove their faith.

But after the fifth Sikh had entered the tent and a fifth thud had been heard, there was a much longer silence and then Guru Gobind Rai came out from his tent – not with his sword but followed by all five Sikhs who had offered up their lives! All were now dressed like the Guru in yellow robes, tied with blue sashes – and each of them was wearing a turban.

'Behold my five brothers,' said the Guru to the crowd who remained. 'These five have passed the hardest test, the test of faith – and they shall be known as the Khalsa, the pure ones. They are soldier saints who will spread abroad the Sikh message of brotherhood and sisterhood.'

And from that time, male Sikhs have not cut their hair but kept it clean and tidy, fastened with a comb under their turbans. And also from that day, they've always worn a steel bracelet as a sign of the one God; and also a tiny sword – as a sign that they are ready to obey the teaching of their faith at all times, just as did the Khalsa that day in Anandpur.

And that day is still remembered by Sikhs each year at the festival of Baisakhi. ◆

49

Hannah Senesh

Hannah Senesh has been called the 'Joan of Arc of Israel': she is a national heroine who has inspired many books and plays and her diary (like that of Anne Frank) has been widely read.

She was a Hungarian Jew who left her homeland in 1939 at the age of eighteen to go to what was then Palestine. Five years later she returned to her native country as a member of an élite volunteer parachute corps, dropped by the British in an attempt to rescue Jews from the Nazi holocaust. Seven of the 32-strong corps were captured, Hannah among them. She was subsequently executed but her courage has remained an inspiration to many.

This is a [another] story about the war, World War II. And it's a true story about a young Jewish woman, Hannah Senesh. She was born in Hungary which [like Holland and many other countries] was under Nazi control during that war. Except that, before the war started, Hannah had left Hungary to go and live in what's now called Israel. At that time it was known as Palestine and was under British command. In many ways, Hannah was quite an ordinary person – but, when the time came, she was extremely brave.

◆

IT ALL BEGAN before the war – in Budapest, the city in Hungary where Hannah grew up. She did well at school. And, as she got a little older, she started earning pocket money by giving lessons to younger children – but then she got a new interest. Up until then of course Hannah had spoken the language of her own country, Hungarian. Now she started learning Hebrew, the traditional language of Jewish people.

And then she got another new interest. At that time, Jewish

people had no country of their own. Indeed, for nearly 2000 years they'd been scattered all over Europe. Arabs lived in what had once been their own Holy Land [back in the time of King David].

But, in the 1930s (just before World War II started), many Jews returned to live in Palestine. They hoped that, one day, at least a part of it might again become their own land.

And in 1939, when Hannah was eighteen, she wrote (in Hebrew) to an agricultural college in Palestine, saying how she wished to learn agriculture and to live and work with Jewish people in Palestine. A little later, she was told she had a place at the college. Then the war started.

Hungary did not join in the fighting at first but its leaders did not wish to upset the German Nazis and life became difficult for the Jews who lived there. [You'll remember from the story of Corrie ten Boom that] the Nazis who then ruled Germany were very anti-Jewish. For example, those Jews who'd owned land had it taken away from them, and when Hannah heard that she'd got her place in agricultural college in Palestine, it was weeks before she was given permission to leave Hungary – just because she was Jewish.

It was a sad occasion at the station when Hannah took leave of her mother and sisters. They had decided to stay in what they thought of as 'home', never expecting it to become really dangerous. If they had known what was going to happen, it would have been an even sadder parting.

The months and years went by. By now, the war had been going on for four long years – with Hannah safe in Palestine, studying and working on the land. But it wasn't so safe for her mother and sisters back in Budapest: by now, Hungary had joined in the war on Germany's side. ☞

Hannah knew that the Jews who were still there were in great danger. And so it was that, just a few years after getting to Palestine, Hannah had the amazing idea that she would go back to Hungary to help her mother and other Jewish people to escape from the Nazis.

The only possible way back into Hungary would be to parachute in. Even that didn't put Hannah off. She joined the British Royal Air Force in Palestine and, with a group of men, she trained as a parachutist.

The plan was that they'd parachute into what was then called Yugoslavia, the country next-door to Hungary, and then cross the border on foot. The men in the group all noticed how brave Hannah was. During the practice jumps, she showed no fear of jumping. And she was fearless about their mission. Never once did she consider they might fail. And in March 1944, when they were told they could go ahead with the plan, she was overjoyed.

Just a few days later they were in Yugoslavia. For months they made their way across that country, in great secrecy. As they got closer to the Hungarian border, news reached them that the German army had now occupied Hungary. It was the first time the men saw Hannah cry. She was crying not just for her mother (to whom almost anything could happen now) but for all of the million Jews in Hungary.

Despite the increased danger, she decided to go on – alone.

She crossed the border safely into Hungary and was hiding in some bushes outside a village when some local farmers saw her and told the police. Only a little while after she'd reached Hungary, she was captured. She was taken by train to Budapest.

Early one morning, her mother, Mrs Catherine Senesh, was surprised when a detective knocked on the door of her flat and insisted she went to the Military Headquarters to be questioned as a 'witness'. She was amazed to discover Hannah was not (as she still thought) at her agricultural college in Palestine but in Budapest – and in prison.

The Germans threatened Hannah that if she didn't reveal her plans, they'd torture her mother before her eyes. Hannah gave nothing away.

The Germans kept them both in the same prison but in separate cells. Just occasionally, during exercise periods, they were able to snatch a few words together. That was all.

The weeks went slowly by, and the war was now coming to an end. The Russians were near Budapest and the Nazis would soon be defeated. Quite suddenly, many of the prisoners, including Hannah's mother, were set free. Hannah was kept in prison.

The charge against her was that she was a British spy. The Germans said she had been found with a radio transmitter and she was obviously a member of the British Armed Forces. They said she had been dropped into Yugoslavia and had made her way into Hungary to rescue British prisoners. She was therefore guilty of major crimes against Hungary and the Germans.

She was found guilty of treason and the death penalty was carried out.

After the war, her body was buried in a Jewish cemetery near Jerusalem in what became Israel, a homeland for Jewish people. But all over the world, Jews still remember Hannah and what she was prepared to do to help her own people. ◆

50

The escape of the Dalai Lama

Tibet was an independent nation for more than 2000 years (the last 300 of them under the rule of the Dalai Lamas) until Chinese Communists swept across the border in 1950 and began a cruel and systematic extermination of the Tibetan culture and Buddhist religion. In 1959 the Dalai Lama and a band of his followers fled to safety in Northern India in order to preserve their culture and religion. In that year more than 400,000 Buddhists in Tibet were put to death.

Tibetans believe that when one Dalai Lama dies his soul is, sometime afterwards, reincarnated in his successor. The present Dalai Lama was born Lhamo Dhondup in 1935. He was brought from a country district to become the leader of his people while a young teenager and he was still only fifteen when his country was invaded by the Chinese. This story raises questions about making difficult choices and 'being a leader'.

What's it like when you're put in charge of something? When you're told to look after your younger brother or sister? How well can you cope?

Suppose, when you're fifteen, you're to be put in charge, not just of one or two people but of a whole country. How will you know what to do? And suppose that country was invaded: then what would you do? Those are some of the questions that faced a Buddhist known as the Dalai Lama who was ruler of a country called Tibet.

(The word 'Lama' means teacher or leader and the word 'Dalai' means ocean; so his name suggests that his knowledge, his wisdom, is as wide and as deep as the ocean.)

◆

FAR, FAR AWAY, to the north of India, are the Himalayan mountains. It's a land of blue skies, and swirling white snow and clouds. It's said to be the 'Roof of the World'! And beyond these mountains is a country called Tibet.

For hundreds of years, little has changed in the streets of Lhasa, the capital city of Tibet. Above all, the people there are peace-loving. They follow the teachings of a man called the Buddha; they're Buddhists.

Some Buddhist men become monks. They wear red or yellow robes and give up all the luxuries of life and live very simply. For hundreds of years, the ruler of Tibet was always one of these monks, who was given the title the Dalai Lama. And the last of these Dalai Lamas is still alive but he now lives not in Tibet but in India.

By the time he was fifteen, he had already become the Dalai Lama. He was the boy ruler of Tibet. But that year, 1949, the communist rulers of next door China announced that they were going to make Tibet part of China. The Chinese army, they said, would march into Tibet! There was nothing the people of Tibet could do to stop them and the following year, the Chinese army *did* march into the Land of the Snows.

The young Dalai Lama knew that there was still much he had to learn about ruling a country. As he said, 'I know nothing about politics!' And there were many difficult decisions he had to make.

But he *was* the religious and political leader of his country. He was 'in charge' – and his people trusted him to know what to do for the best.

For nine years, he tried to make peace with the Chinese but gradually they took over more and more of his country. They built roads so that their troops could move about easily. They destroyed many temples and monasteries where the monks ☞

lived. They tried to stop everyone from being Buddhists – but still the Dalai Lama hoped to save his people and their faith in the way of the Buddha. What's more, he hoped to do this without violence (because, like all Buddhists, he believed violence was always wrong).

However, many Tibetans were becoming impatient at the way the Chinese were interfering in their country. Some of them started to try to fight the Chinese.

The Chinese fought back. They moved more troops to Lhasa. Then the Tibetan people began to fear that the Chinese might kidnap or even kill their Dalai Lama. Indeed, many thought it best that he should leave the country, so as to be safe. He himself wasn't sure. He didn't want to run away and leave his people. But he understood their fears. If he was killed or taken prisoner by the Chinese, that would be the end of Tibet. It would no longer be a separate country but just part of China. But if he did escape, if he did 'run away', perhaps one day, he could return and rule Tibet in peace again.

So that was his choice. What should he decide to do? Stay with his people and risk being killed? Or save himself in the hope that one day he might return? Not an easy choice.

He thought it all over and over and reluctantly he decided he should leave the country.

The escape of the Dalai Lama from Tibet had, of course, to be kept a secret from the Chinese army. So he and a small group of his followers made their plans in the greatest secrecy.

First, they disguised themselves: no longer did they wear their red and yellow monks' robes, but the ordinary rough clothes of Tibetan soldiers. The Dalai Lama even wore a rifle over his shoulder, to complete the disguise.

The night they planned to escape, there was a sand storm. It could not have come at a better time – because it hid them from the Chinese.

They had no trouble leaving the Dalai Lama's house, crossing the garden and then walking along the bed of a dried-up river. Once they were outside the city, they found ponies waiting for them, just as had been planned. Everything was going well. Quickly they mounted. To the right were the lights of a Chinese camp. They were terrified the noise of the ponies' hooves on the stony path would alert the Chinese. But luckily all the Chinese heard was the noise of the storm.

Their route led up through the mountains. The paths were narrow and difficult and they often had to dismount and lead the ponies in the darkness. Then, in the morning, as the sun rose, a stranger suddenly appeared and offered the Dalai Lama a white horse on which to ride. They continued, more easily now, over the summit, down into a valley, and through villages where other people joined them. But news came that the Chinese had destroyed the Dalai Lama's home and would be certain to kill him if they found him.

Now he knew it was right to leave Tibet and make for the safety of India – even though the journey would take many days, perhaps even a month.

But then the weather worsened. Heavy snow bit into their faces. Then brilliant sunlight reflected off the snow and threatened to blind those who had no goggles. They slept at night in makeshift tents and, by day, struggled on, across hills and frozen desert plains. There were dust storms and later torrential rain. One night the Dalai Lama's tent leaked so badly that he was forced to sit up shivering all night. He became very ill but there could be no waiting till he got better. Reports of Chinese ☛

troops in the neighbourhood forced them to move on – until at last they crossed into India and safety.

More than 40 years have since gone by and still the peace-loving Dalai Lama has not been able to return to Tibet. But perhaps the day is not too far distant when once again the Dalai Lama will be able to return in peace to his people. ◆